Good Night Kendrick,

I Love You

Good Night Kendrick, I Love You

I Love You

A MOTHER'S JOURNAL THROUGH GRIEF

Rhonda Roseland Fincher

Order this book online at www.trafford.com
or email orders@trafford.com

Most Trafford titles are also available at major online book retailers.

Cover design by Matt Langevin
Author photo courtesy of Amber Morrison

Printed in the United States of America.

ISBN: 978-1-4269-5389-7 (sc)
ISBN: 978-1-4269-5388-0 (hc)
ISBN: 978-1-4269-5390-3 (e)

Library of Congress Control Number: 2011900190

Trafford rev. 01/17/2011

 www.trafford.com

North America & international
toll-free: 1 888 232 4444 (USA & Canada)
phone: 250 383 6864 ♦ fax: 812 355 4082

To:

My children Kendrick, Keegan, Rylee, and Brennan--you are the biggest blessings and joy of my life.

My parents, John and Darlene Roseland--you provided me with the guidance and direction to know it is not the things in life that matter, but the love and generosity we share with others.

The parents who share the experience of losing a child--may you find comfort in knowing the challenges are real and you are not alone.

God, grant me the serenity
to accept the things I cannot change;
courage to change the things I can;
and wisdom to know the difference.

(Reinhold Niebuhr)

CONTENTS

Introduction

My son died in 1995 and I found comfort in reading books on grief and writing letters to him. Kendrick had heat stroke at his first day of football practice on August 7, 1995. For the next 18 days we watched as he lay in a drug-induced coma fighting for his life. On August 25, 1995 he died from multi-system organ failure as a result of heat stroke. We knew of families that had lost children. I worked with a lady once that lost her two-year-old daughter to meningitis. I remember wondering how she could be so strong and come back to work after only one week. After losing a child, I still wonder; however, I do know that we each grieve differently. Some of us are buoyed by our faith, friends, and previous challenges that have given us insight to get us through. Some of us crumble to pieces and have to rebuild our lives from the shattered fragments of what used to be our lives. I crumbled, but I was able to rebuild a life and you can, too.

Grief is all-encompassing. Grief is hard. Grief will pass. Yes, I did say that. Grief will pass. The sadness will be there, the memories will be there, the ache will be there. But, the all-encompassing grief will pass. You may be at a stage where you don't even want the pain to pass. There is a time when you want to hold on to the grief because that is all you feel you have of your child. The grief is what connects you to your child and you nurture it for all it is worth. And then, a time will come when you feel you are able to release the grief. Like a child who turns 18—you don't want to release them into the world but the time has come and it is time for them to go on their way. So it is with grief. The time will come when you feel you can release it and let something else replace the grief in your heart.

Allow grief to be a part of your life. Embrace it instead of allowing it to engulf you and immobilize you. Read, learn, share, get counseling, and allow your friends and family to support you. And then, as your heart heals, allow the aching and empty spots to be filled with something else that will heal you and make you whole again.

Will the road be easy? No, it will not. You will have to force yourself to live and going through the motions of life will be a challenge. Finding ways to help you lessen the pain will make living easier. One of the ways I coped with my grief was through writing letters to Kendrick. After some years I realized that my journals may help another grieving parent. There are many books on grief, but none that I could find that chronicled the grief during the process. You have heard that misery loves company. I believe that your pain may be lessened by knowing that others feel the same pain and do survive. So, here I am many years later finally having the courage and strength to share my letters to Kendrick with you.

I considered leaving out sections of the journal that I wasn't sure I should put in that might be perceived as negative. I considered changing some of the wording to make it sound softer. What I realized is that in order to help grieving parents, I needed to stay true to what I wrote many years ago when I was in the turmoil of grief. My friend, Brandi, who lost her son, Tyler, said after reading this, "I just thought I was mean." Now she doesn't feel so alone in her grief and better understands that others might feel the same way.

Background

Kendrick was born on a cold night in Grand Forks, North Dakota, on February 5, 1982. He was two weeks overdue and didn't quite want to leave the warmth of my womb. After over ten hours of labor he was pulled out with forceps and greeted the world at 8 pounds 13 ounces with a large bump on his head from the forceps. I cried all day when I went back to work after eight weeks home with him. My boss told me to go home and I said, "I have to do this sometime so I might as well get through it."

Kendrick grew quickly and was always large for his age. He always loved anything to do with sports, from playing baseball with Grandpa Roseland in the backyard when he was still in diapers to starting recreational sports when he was in elementary school. We always let him try the sports he wanted and never forced him into any sport. He had played t-ball, soccer, baseball, basketball and was looking forward to playing football when he started eighth grade. We were living in California when Kendrick told me he wanted to play football when he started eighth grade. I just said, "Yes, that will be fine."

When Kendrick was almost five we moved to Colorado for his dad's job. He attended first grade in Boulder and second through fifth grades in Littleton. When Kendrick was seven we had another child, Keegan, and Kendrick was a doting (okay, and teasing) older brother. When Kendrick was eleven we moved to California for my job. We lived in Pleasanton during Kendrick's sixth and seventh grades and moved to

Arkansas for my job in March of his seventh grade. On the day he registered for his new school in March 1995, 6'2" 220 pound Kendrick was followed out of school by the football coach. Of course, that is just what Kendrick wanted. He went to summer football camp and the rest is a history I wish I could rewrite.

Note to Readers

When reading this book, note that my words to you are in regular print and my letters to Kendrick are in italics.

Chapter 1

Dear God, Not My Child!

I am selfish. I do not want my child to die. Other people lose children, but not me. Surely God cares enough about me, enough about Kendrick, that he will not take him from me. For those of us who did not have a child die instantly, we plead, we beg, we bargain. We bargained for 18 days. Those were long days in some ways, but also short because they were the final days we could spend with him. When we were in the hospital I began writing notes so that when Kendrick got out he would be able to read what happened during his stay. The day of Kendrick's heat stroke, I was in Atlanta for a meeting. I think I had a premonition or something because I really did not want to go to Atlanta. In fact, the night before, while I was packing, I had this strange feeling and I remember walking from the bedroom into the family room where Kendrick was watching television. I said, "I hate that I have to leave for this meeting."

He chuckled and said, "But Mom, it is only two days." I said, "I know, Honey, but I will miss you and I always want to be with you."

These are the notes from our 18 days of hope and hell.

August 7, 1995 – Monday

Daddy called me at 5:00 p.m. in Atlanta and said you'd had an accident at football. It was amazing he reached me because I had just stepped into the hotel room to drop off my luggage and head back down to meet everyone for dinner. When Daddy told me you had an accident, I was thinking, "Oh no, he broke something on his first day of practice." I said, "What did he break?" Dad said you had a heat stroke. I didn't really know that it was so bad and I said, "So, do you want me to come home?"

Daddy kind of chuckled that 'you're crazy' chuckle and said, "Yes." So then I figured it was pretty serious because he wouldn't have told me to come home otherwise. He said you were in ICU because of your size.

I left the hotel at 5:30 p.m. for a 6:40 flight. The others at the meeting said I would never make it on that flight, but God cleared the road because I made it to the car rental return in an hour and to the gate with five minutes to spare. It was the last flight out that day to Arkansas. I called the hospital on the airplane and found out you were being airlifted to Little Rock Children's Hospital so I was able to change my ticket when I changed planes in Memphis to go to Little Rock versus Fayetteville.

I made it to the hospital about 45 minutes before the helicopter. That was a very long 45 minutes. They let me ride up in the elevator with you but then they shooed me away and I didn't get to see you for another three hours. I had a lot of fretting time. I had them call the chaplain. Pastor Sidney came and talked with me and prayed with me. I felt bad "begging" God to heal you when it seems I'm always just asking for things. Pastor Sidney, the chaplain on duty, said he believes God allows our lives to be lived within a set of parameters and that God doesn't intend for anything bad to happen to his children. I said, "I'm sure there is a purpose in this and I don't believe it is that Kendrick should die."

August, 9, 1995 — Wednesday

Daddy and I traded places at 4 a.m. When I got to your room you were steadily going downhill. Your nurse was having a tough time. I remember it was 4:30 a.m. and she stood there and said, "I'm so confused."

I prayed, "Dear God, just let Kendrick hold on until 7 a.m. when new nurses can help." Sometime that morning your body went into shock. The first thing that happened was your kidneys stopped working.

I remember the doctor telling me that morning, "You know, there is a very real chance that he may die." That was about 6:30 a.m. One of the people from the Atlanta meeting had told me where she would be staying in Little Rock on business and that I could call if I needed anything. You might remember her because she worked in Denver with me when we lived there—Tammy Murabito. I called her and asked if she could watch Keegan until Grandpa Fincher arrived. She brought some items I needed and came over with games and some things for Keegan and comic books for you. I can't wait for you to read them. I called Daddy after I talked to my friend Tammy and told him he needed to come back so he got up and he was here by 8 a.m.

Grandpa Fincher and Cindy (Grandpa Fincher's wife) and Tammy arrived around 8:30 a.m.

This was a real waiting and praying day. Another patient's grandpa and I were visiting and he said he knew a lady that was having failure of all her vital organs and she didn't have a chance to live.

The Mormon Church elders came in and anointed her with oil and blessed her and she fully recovered. He said to let him know if I wanted them to come in for you. So, later that afternoon I asked if they could and he rounded up two elders plus himself and they came and blessed you that evening. They said they had a great feeling about you as they were blessing you. They said they never felt so good about an individual and that they believed you were going to survive and accomplish great things in your life.

We were not attending church regularly at the time; however, I am Christian and not a believer in the Mormon doctrine. At the time, I wanted to grasp at whatever might help Kendrick survive. After listening to this new friend tell me about how someone else survived with little chance and attributing it to the anointing, I wanted to see if it could help Kendrick.

The doctors told us they didn't think you would survive the night. Dad had to tell Keegan and she cried and cried so we just held her till she cried herself to sleep. Grandma Roseland's (my mother) airplane flight was delayed and she ended up on a bus from Memphis. We were concerned you may not make it until she arrived.

August 10, 1995 – Thursday

6:30 a.m. –Your blood pressure has been dropping all night and they were having trouble stabilizing you. They were pumping shots of medicine, saline and plasma in you to bring your blood pressure to a higher reading. The doctor said at 6:30 that there wasn't any more they could do. We were all called into your room— Grandpa Fincher, Grandma Roseland and Aunt Sheryl (his dad's sister) who had both arrived overnight, me and Dad—we were standing around your bed and they pulled the curtains closed around us. I guess we were supposed to say goodbye and they were giving us some privacy, but none of us could say goodbye. We just prayed and cried.

I couldn't understand—I just knew that this wasn't supposed to be happening.

Soon your blood pressure started going up on its own into the 60's and then the doctors and nurses started coming back in and checking you over. They then continued to treat you with fluids and medicine and your blood pressure kept improving. About an hour later your nurse said, "I can stop this at any time." We asked if what they were doing was futile and she thought maybe it was futile and just prolonging death. We asked the doctor and he said it wasn't futile and he would let us know if he felt it was.

The mother of the girl in the next room who has cerebral palsy came and gave me a hug and said she was praying for you and us. She said, "I feel bad for you because I know you're not used to this and we are." The RN kept giving me hugs too. I remember being so weak and so tired and I sat in a chair outside your room crying and leaning on Grandma. I just wanted to sleep and wake up and find you okay.

Grandma had arrived about 3 a.m. today. We weren't sure you were even going to be alive when she got here. Tammy stayed and made sure Grandma got picked up and brought her here and then Tammy waited here until this afternoon. She sure has been a blessing.

Sue Cauthen and Sharon Wolfe arrived this afternoon (friends from Rogers).

August 11, 1995 – Friday

At 2 a.m. there was an overhead page for the parents of Kendrick Fincher to report to ICU. They told us you needed dialysis and *thought you would go into cardiac arrest. The doctors took us into the conference room and then we waited in the quiet room.*

By 2 p.m. you were fairly stable and they told us we needed to start following regular visiting hours. That was okay with us because we loved to hear that you were getting better.

Sharon Wolfe and Sue Cauthen left because Sue had to work. It was so nice to have them here with us during the night.

When the doctors called us in that conference room to tell us that dialysis was needed, I was very tired of them telling us that Kendrick could die. I just wanted to hear that they were treating him and that he would survive. It felt like they thought his fight for survival was futile, and I told them that I just wanted them to treat him like a patient that was going to survive.

August 16, 1995 – Wednesday

Dad woke me up at 2 a.m. and said, "We need to talk." We went to the transport room and he started telling me that your heart was weak . . .

I said, "Wait a minute, let me get Mom because she will pray while we worry." Your heart was beating at about 50 beats per minute and your blood pressure was in the 70's. The doctor doesn't know what is causing this except that your heart is tired.

Positives overnight were that some of your signs are improving. I was so worried all morning that I told the doctor I would be in the waiting room because I couldn't handle it. There was a short time when you were awake slightly. It was like having a new baby. We got Grandma Roseland and Grandpa Fincher and we all were talking to you—so excited about a minor tongue or neck movement.

They started dialysis about 11 a.m. today and that seemed to help your overall picture. Your blood pressure went up and your heart is attempting to stabilize. I was talking to the doctor and I said you have jumped over so many hurdles already and I'm praying and hoping that you can jump a couple more and he said, "He will!!" Now, I am surprised he said you can make it since they tend to give us such bad news. I am so excited that the doctors now believe you can be okay.

We've only played the tapes to you a couple times today. Your day nurse likes you to have quiet time and she dims the lights and turns off all noise. You are such a special child. I'm really missing your smile, kind words, I love you's, and even your teasing! My heart just drops now as I think about how much I long to hear you say, "I love you" again.

The tapes we played for Kendrick were ones I recorded to play for him when I couldn't be in the room holding his hand.

More people called today. When I needed an angel this morning to comfort me a lady that knows some mutual friends called to see how you are. She said she was thinking about you and praying. I told Grandma that I knew you'd be okay as that was a sign to me. The pastor from a local church also called for an update. The school secretary called from school, and also some friends and your Aunt Rochelle (my sister) called. You received another balloon today—that makes 24 now. We also received another two goodie baskets. Grandma said she could just picture you digging though the baskets.

I can't wait to hear you say again—"Good night, Mom, I love you!" and give me a good night kiss. You are always so sweet. You have been fairly stable, or at least the doctors aren't too concerned this afternoon and evening. I guess they believe your heart is trying to become regulated. I've prayed for God to help you through the night and keep your heart rate and blood pressure where the doctors would like to see it. God has already answered so many prayers.

Grandma and I just went to the chapel to pray for you and your healing. I prayed that the doctors and nurses will be guided. That's what I prayed the day they did the first dialysis and were fearful that you wouldn't tolerate it.

Grandpa Fincher, Cindy, Keegan and Coquet went to our house today. They decided they would go hold down the fort and Grandpa is really stressed about you. Me too, but I know you need me here and if you can be strong, I can too. We both have to be strong together to help you get well.

I'm hoping to get a good night sleep and that means that you'll have a good night if I get to sleep. I've been scared to sleep since Daddy woke me up this morning. You are so precious to me. I hope everybody in the world is hugging their kids more. I can't wait to get another hug from you. I love you! Sleep well and get well tonight dear baby. I'm waiting for you to open your eyes so I can look into them and tell you how much I love you and I'm praying tomorrow may be the day. You continue to be awesome—Kendrick the Conqueror.

August 17, 1995 – Thursday

9:30 a.m. - I woke at 11:45 p.m. last night worried about you so I got up and went to the chapel and prayed. I was awake for about an hour thinking about you. I was so happy when I went down to see you at 5 a.m. and Dad said you had been pretty stable the last few hours. Your heart rate is now rhythmic which is excellent. They have decreased another blood pressure medicine slightly and the peep on the ventilator was also reduced.

Rose Peterson (a friend of ours from Minnesota) and Aunty Sheryl called this morning. Dad talked to Sheryl, but we were out when Rose called. Keegan called to talk to us too. I guess she was pretty lonesome last night without us. She said Tiger (a cat that visited our house) was waiting on Dad's pickup for her. She said Tiger slept with Grandpa.

7 p.m. – Your stats have been good all afternoon. It is so nice to see you maintaining. You know I never have liked roller coaster rides. Your nurse changed your tubes and she said you didn't like it at all. In fact your blood pressure went up, which was good, since usually it goes down when you get upset.

I talked with a friend from Colorado today. She said a kid from her high school in North Dakota died from heat stroke years ago. Nothing was ever done. Another boy in Chicago also had heatstroke last Saturday. We're going to make sure people know about heat stroke now, Honey!! And we're going to make sure schools are accountable for prevention.

We're able to have a room at Ronald McDonald's House now. It is pretty nice. Daddy sleeps during the day. Grandma and I are still sleeping in the waiting room because we don't like to be too far away. We got the tapes from Grandpa Roseland today that he had recorded about his childhood and you got to listen to histories again. I'm sure you can hear.

It seems like we've been here for so long and it's been one long day. I can't seem to keep the days straight.

At this point, we had been in the hospital 12 continuous days and had not left for anything except to walk to the Ronald McDonald House a block away. The only changes were Kendrick's condition, the coming and going of different staff and patients, what was served in the cafeteria, and the click of the clock which really didn't matter. The only thing that mattered was Kendrick's condition.

August 19, 1995 – Saturday

You had a good night last night, but today has been up and down. Your blood pressure drops and they have to give you fluids and plasma to get it up. I get so nervous when I am in there and when I'm not in there I'm nervous and I hardly dare walk in. I just want someone to go in and tell me you are okay and then I'll dare go in.

This was Mike's and my 17th wedding anniversary. Usually my mom and I took shifts with Kendrick together, slept on the same shift and ate together and Mike took the alternating shift. This day, my mom told Mike and I to go have dinner together in the cafeteria. It was very thoughtful of my mother to help make sure we spent time together on our anniversary, even though Kendrick was the primary concern of all of us.

August 20, 1995 – Sunday

Today I am very emotional over this roller coaster ride you have us on. Your blood pressure has been all over the place. It was as low as 49 and as high as 185 all because of fluid volume. But the worst shifts were due to a machine pause early this morning and then they had to double pump your medicine and that sent it so high. When they told me that your pupils were unequal tonight I was concerned that your blood pressure changes had caused a problem. But the doctor said not to worry as long as you were still responsive. Usually they give us the worst news, so if he says not to worry then I know I don't need to. But anyhow, I prayed for your mind just in case.

I couldn't go to sleep tonight without talking to you so I made another tape for you. I gave it to Duddy to play in the night time if needed. Darell Floyd (a friend that I worked with in Rogers) and his son Kenni came by on their way back from Dallas. He came in to visit you and I could tell it was emotional for him. He's been a great help at work taking care of work for me.

I call Sandy Miller (friend from work that hired me in Denver and then was living in Chicago) every day with the Kendrick report and she passes it on to other work people. Some days I'm scared to report because your condition changes so quickly.

August 21, 1995 – Monday

4:25 p.m. You have had a great day today!! They have reduced your medicine and you tolerated that well. We were just talking to you and you would blink and move your head. You coughed when the respiratory therapist asked you to. It was pretty exciting to have you responding.

They increased your formula to 20 cc per hour. That's twice what you were getting on Saturday. So soon they will be seeing if your bowels are functioning and you will start having a mess! You better get well soon!

You have one of our favorite nurses as your nurse again today. She has been taking very good care of you. They didn't even have to dialyze today—just the small machine. So your lab reports are looking better.

An eleven year old across the hall from you died today from meningitis. I'm very sad for his family but in the same breath I thank God that you are alive. We are so fortunate that you're the fighter that you are and that so many people are praying for you.

Kendrick the Conqueror.

I still feel guilty that I was so focused on Kendrick's condition that the thought of another child dying just brought me thankfulness that my child was alive.

5:10 p.m. They were just here to take your picture for the Associated Press release. Like I've been telling you, Sweetie, you will make a difference in people's lives. No one should have to suffer like you have.

The patient whose grandparents have been keeping us company here gets to move to a regular room now. He's much better. His mom, aunt, and grandpa have been so good to us here and we've enjoyed their company. His grandpa is the one who gathered the elders of the Mormon Church for your blessing last week. Or, I guess that was the week before—it was Wednesday, the 9th.

Daddy said he talked to you most of the night because you seemed so alert.

August 22, 1995 – Tuesday

You had another good day today!

August 23, 1995 – Wednesday

11 p.m. I'm having a tough time today. I guess you're doing the same but my emotions are shot. Your blood pressure was low when

I came in at 6:30 this morning and so I started off worried. I think I need to just cry for awhile. They've given you extra platelets and plasma today and reduced your medicine so actually you're better than yesterday. I'm just not!!

Your feeding tube was not positioned all the way into your intestines, which they had to x-ray to determine. So they gave you some medicine to contract your stomach and move it down. It appears that worked.

They also have to put in a new arterial line because the new one they put in your right arm a few days ago is not reading your blood pressure correctly. They were in the middle of it and they had another emergency so they had to stop. They've also taken your ventilator off twice and did manual breaths so they could suction you out better. I get too nervous when they do that so I had to leave. But, then I sent Grandma in because I think someone should be with you.

I'm sitting here very angry at the coach and wondering why he's enjoying his life and still has his job. I just tried to call the lawyer to check on the investigation but there wasn't an answer.

It is normal to want to get answers and to have someone to be angry at. We wanted to know what happened at football practice that day and find out if the coaches did anything improperly. There were all sorts of reports coming to us that we found disturbing and we had called the county prosecutor's office to have it investigated.

I guess your lungs are still cloudy and they don't like that, but your liver is still showing signs of improvement, no new infections. When you wake up you won't be able to move. You will need extensive physical therapy. The doctor says you may also need a tracheotomy put in temporarily because you've been on the ventilator so long.

They are keeping you very sedated and still so you don't move or get excited. It's easier for them to maintain your vitals when you aren't moving.

That was the end of my postings from the hospital. Kendrick died two days later on August 25th and our hope of his survival ended. There will be more notes about his last hours, the funeral, and other moments in the journal entries during the days ahead.

Chapter 2

My World Has Stopped

Why are the nurses laughing? Why are the people driving? Why do people go to work? Can't they see my child has died? Can't they see that the world has stopped turning? What is this rush about? Why does it matter what we eat, what we wear, what kind of car we drive, what we are doing? How will I ever work again? How will I ever laugh again? How can I live?

When your child dies or you lose anyone close to you, those are your first thoughts. Of course, Kendrick had died and there wasn't any reason to write any more to him. He was never going to be able to read about his stay in Children's Hospital. However, soon the pain was so great and I had to write to him. I had to feel close to him. I had to share my thoughts with him. So, when we returned from Minnesota on September 9, 1995—after a funeral in Arkansas and a funeral in Minnesota—I started writing to my child in heaven. This was a very painful time. Some call it shock or denial. I don't really care what it is called. I just know my world had stopped and the only way I could deal with life was by letting it pull me where it needed. I could not function and I had no desire to function. Writing to Kendrick was my connection to my child. Because this may help you, another grieving parent, I share these writings with you.

September 9, 1995

Today was our first day back from Minnesota. We got back about 11:30 p.m. last night. We debated staying somewhere and coming back in daylight as nights are so hard to face anyhow. But . . . we came back. We left everything in the car except our toiletries bag and your remains. I remember when we picked "the box" up from Green funeral home on Thursday. Daddy said, "All that's left fits in a box," and we cried.

We had Kendrick cremated because we were not sure if we would want him buried in Arkansas or Minnesota and we did not know where we would end up living down the road. We did not want our child buried somewhere we would not be able to visit the gravesite. I remember growing up that there had been some controversy over Christians being cremated and I talked with my dad about it. He said that there was no place in the Bible that prohibited it and that his main concern was that we had a memorial stone so he wasn't forgotten about in generations to come. There is a little church a few miles from where I grew up and where my parents still live and Kendrick's memorial stone is there. His remains are in a brass box with his photo on it in my living room with two special angel figurines given to us by Grandpa Fincher by its side.

We've been crying so much. We miss you so. This morning we opened many, many cards. We cried lots. But, you know, it feels better to cry than to be totally numb. We were in a daze all day. We only left to get the mail--or Dad did. Keegan and I were home all day. It was 7 p.m. before I realized we hadn't eaten all day. Grandma called and so did Aunt Robin (my sister—I can't believe I haven't mentioned her sooner! She was at home in Minnesota with six-month old twins during all this!). *Sandy Miller called too. Every day I wonder how I will ever live this life without you. I know you were jealous of your sister, but I'm so glad she's here.*

She's been a great comfort. She comes and puts her arms around me when I'm crying. I love you, my baby!

September 10, 1995

A restless night. I had the urge to go visit your room during the night but I don't like going downstairs during the day let alone the night. So I waited until 7 a.m. I went through your drawers and just touched your stuff. Then I went through the papers you'd cleaned out of your room a couple months ago. I found some real special papers, especially the Mother's Day card to me from 1992. It made me feel good. I know we had a special bond, Sweetheart, and I hope our spirits keep that bond until we meet again in heaven. Keegan got to play with her friend at our house and at her friend's house today. When her mom dropped her off I couldn't hold back my tears as we visited. She lost a brother to cancer three years ago and went into a deep depression. He was 52—you only got 13 ½ years. I'm so glad I had the pleasure of having you for my son!! Keegan got to see the neighbor's kitties yesterday. She was pretty excited about that. We went to church at First Baptist this morning. We were late because they moved the time to 10:30 from 10:50. We enjoy going there. I wish you were here and we were all going together, but maybe we would have continued to procrastinate if you were still here. Now, we want to worship God and join you in heaven.

September 11, 1995

Today Keegan went back to school. When I went to pick her up I had a strong urge to drive to Elmwood and pretend you were still here and visualize you coming out of school like all the other kids. But, I didn't—I came home and cried. We visited the lawyer today. I hope he and his partner will do well for you. We also got the plans for your ball field from Grandpa Fincher. They look great.

It is normal to want to have a legacy for your child and make sure people don't forget they lived. Your child will always live on in your heart, but having something tangible that you can talk about, see and touch makes you believe you can keep their memory alive. One of the first things we talked about was doing a baseball park in Kendrick's memory because baseball was his favorite sport.

> *Keegan wrote a note for you. Today the young lady that wrote the poem for you came over after school to meet us. She is very nice. She said you had a girlfriend and we are wondering who that is. We think it may have been the girl from next door.*

After the funeral in Arkansas there was a poem that was left in Kendrick's casket by a classmate, Kristy Oldham, from his school. It read,

> We miss you Kendrick our hearts are sore
> Each day we miss you more and more
> Your friendly smile, your gentle face
> No one could ever take your place
> Until memory fades and life departs
> You will live forever within our hearts.

We loved this poem and we had it engraved on the back of his memorial stone and his urn.

> *Green Funeral Home found a place in Chicago that will engrave your urn. We have to get a black and white photo, though, rather than color. We picked up your death certificate today. It looks a lot like a birth certificate. I wish children didn't have to die and I guess I'm selfish and especially wish you didn't leave us. We so much wanted to see you get well and see you grow into an adult. You brought so much joy into our lives. While we were walking tonight I was thinking that we were fortunate to have you even if only for 13 1/2 years. Some people can't have children and never know the*

joy of children. Not only can we have children, but we had you for 13 ½ years and we exchanged so much love and have so many great memories. I guess I have a lot to be thankful for because I had you here and we'll be able to have you with us again in eternity. There is so much I want to talk to you about. This helps, although I'd rather be holding your hand or looking in your eyes. As I write I feel peaceful, like I'm with your soul. I need lots of comfort from you and God. I pray that you will help God bless us. You know we have had many challenges, but this has been the biggest we have ever had. Daddy and I have wanted to die so we can be with you, but we have Keegan and our families here. They are all very sad over your death from this earth. We have wondered if we should have more children. If we are going to be here another fifty years, then I'd like more joy around. Even if we aren't, I'd like more family in heaven. So, what do you think we should do? Do you want more brothers or sisters? I bet if you were in earthly form, you'd say no, but I wonder now what you would say.

I think I may try to go in to work this week. We have been in a daze mostly. Daddy has actually been watching television. I asked him if he was trying to take your place and he said no, he was just trying to check out the Karma. We signed up for basic cable today. We want to watch any news reports so we know what they are saying in the media. If/when we sue, it will be on the news and we want to hear the reports. We meet with the prosecutor on Wednesday morning. The attorney thinks they are trying for negligent homicide but they don't believe they will be able to convict on that even. Even that is only a misdemeanor with up to one year in jail and a $1,000 fine. You were such a wonderful young man. It makes me so angry that these coaches caused your death—we no longer have you here and that is no crime as far as our legal system is concerned. We do not believe it is appropriate for us to prosper personally from your death; however, we believe the school, coaches and community need to realize the wrong that has been done.

*Well, Honey, I'll say good night. I miss your "Good night, Mom,
I love you's."*

At this point, we were still looking for answers, as all we knew was that
we had sent our healthy son to football practice and he died.

September 12, 1995

*Last night was hard again. I remember being awake for a long time
and I had an urge to go outside—maybe so I'd be closer to you.
It was 4:30 a.m. and I went out on the deck and it was starting
to rain. It was raining when I took Keegan to school too. I was
thinking about a song that was out a few years ago that talked
about "washing the pain." I wish I could wash away the pain.
The only way to do that is to have you back. I went to the library
today and got some grieving books and one life after death book. I
just can't believe you are gone. I called Grandma tonight because
I was worried about her. I don't know what to do, though. I feel
so badly myself I can't really comfort anyone else. We have so many
caring friends, but I still feel so alone. I talked to Sue Cauthen
tonight and she said Derrick* (Kendrick's best buddy in Arkansas
and Sue's son) *really misses you too. I cannot believe this sorrow
that we have to bear. I pray that you have a mansion in heaven
and that you're very happy. I was thinking that Great Grandma
Roseland is in heaven and she's probably telling you a bunch of
stories about Grandpa Roseland. Even though you don't get to listen
to Grandpa's stories here you'll get to hear them.*

*I hope we find a purpose to all this suffering. I can't imagine what
purpose could be great enough to justify losing you.*

*Daddy wasn't feeling well today. He has a sinus cold and
headache.*

I'm spending a lot more time with Keegan now. Doing a lot of the things I wish I could do with you—reading, walking, beads—we'd do Legos or cards. I really miss playing Scrabble and cards with you.

Daddy was asking today if we should still buy you Christmas presents. I said I didn't think I could handle any more reminders that you aren't here. I'd like to do some Christmas activities in your memory like adopt a family. I wish you were here to give you that leather bomber jacket you wanted. That was going to be your present and I was so looking forward to seeing you open and wear it. I knew you'd be so excited.

Kendrick, you and God need to help us make the right decisions on so many things we have to do. We want to make a difference in this world so your death is not in vain. Even though you aren't here in physical body, we want people to know you. You had a lot of admirers here and I hope you'll be a role model even through your death.

One day closer to heaven—Good night, Kendrick – I love you.

September 14, 1995

Hi Sweetie. I didn't get to write to you yesterday because Sue Cauthen (Derrick's mom) came at 7 p.m. to help me write thank you notes. She stayed until 1 a.m. and we didn't get any thank you notes done! We had a nice visit. I needed to talk to someone. The last two days have been the worst I think. Yesterday I was very depressed. My boss called, which was good because I was really sinking into despair. He called the pastor and the employee assistance line. The pastor really didn't have much to say but he did give my name to a lady with Compassionate Friends and she called today. She said it only gets worse. I know I can't accept nor handle that! Her son died in 1980. Today when Daddy left me alone for about 45 minutes I thought I was going to go mad. I yelled for you and cried for you—"Kendrick where are you? God, why did you take my boy?" I am in so much pain. It is hard to think or do anything.

I went in to work for about 2 ½ hours today. I thought it was time I begin to move on. It felt good to be at the office, but I felt like I was letting go, and yet I want to hang on to my grief and pain because that makes me feel a little closer to you.

Kristi Oldham came over again today. We visited lots and she had pizza with us and then we took her home. She is a nice girl. Your "girlfriend," Aileah Righter, called yesterday. You had never mentioned her so we were wondering who she is. We called Derrick and he doesn't know who she is either.

I feel so alone. People really aren't calling—it seems everybody has forgotten about our sorrow. I have to read Billy Graham's book on life after death next so I can better know what your new life is like.

Keegan is picking out boy and girl names. She wants a brother and a sister. I can't really tell how she's taking your death. Seems she's taking it too well. Like I was for awhile and still do at times—total denial! I just can't believe you're gone sometimes. You were so alive one moment, so helpless and fragile the next, and gone from our lives forever the next.

One day at a time . . . but when will I be able to be happy again, or carefree? I was wondering if I would ever feel like dancing again. When will I be motivated to clean, cook, work and other ordinary day-to-day activities? I just want to read, mourn, and write to you. Oh, I like to spend lots of time with Keegan. It is such a blessing we have her. If God had planned taking you at age 13 ½, no wonder we got our additional blessing because Daddy and I would have found a peaceful way to die along with you. Life would not have anything to hold us here.

Jennifer Cingolani (friend of mine from work) came over from work about 5 yesterday and stayed until 7. That helped me decide to go to work today, too. She listened to me and cried with me. I so need to talk to people but I'm not sure I want to talk to others who grieve. I need comfort myself.

The newspapers have sure been reporting a lot of lies about your death. I finally read some tonight. But, of course, the school is trying to protect themselves. I can't wait for the truth to be known. I don't want your death to be in vain. We have to make a difference for you. Please, you and God guide us. We may not be making the right decisions in our despair. I look at your pictures and I miss you so and wonder how I will ever survive this life without you.

Life is cruel, so cruel! What will I do? Where do I go from here?

Good night, Kendrick. I love you, I miss you.

September 15, 1995

Hi Honey. Well, today was three weeks since you died so it's been almost six weeks since you had the accident. I did much better today. I prayed last night for some peace about your death because the last week has been so painful. The pain is almost a physical pain. It's hard to describe. But now you can see our souls so you can sense our pain. Some thoughts I've been thinking that comfort me and that I was talking about to my friend Lois Holt in Salt Lake City are these: 1) You are in a place of no pain and suffering, 2) I was so fortunate to have you as my child for 13 ½ years, 3) some people don't even get the joy of having children, 4) we are never promised another day, 5) I'd rather have had you for 13 ½ years than not at all, 6) we gave you lots of love and I know that you know you were and are loved, 7) too many things went wrong—God must have really wanted you, 8) God's plan was being carried out and God knew when he gave us our little unplanned Keegan that we would need her as a comforter when he took you in a few years.

Well, those are some thoughts that have helped. It sure beats going crazy!! I even got the name of a therapist today. I didn't call, though. Today I did okay. I think I'll take advantage of the service at some time since it's provided by work and even though I'm okay today, I may not be in a week or a month.

I saw a profound statement at Keegan's school:
    Yesterday was
    Today is
    Tomorrow will be
It seems strange that life goes on. In our house it feels like time stopped so it is good to get out. We are forcing ourselves to get busy so we don't get mired in depression. We have so much to do in your name. We have so much to do to help us do all the good we want to accomplish. I wonder how much time we have. Now you know. You are so smart—just like I always told you!

Will I get a good night's sleep? I always wake up with fear in the early a.m. It's a panic fear. My beautiful, kind son.

I sure am sleepy. It is 1 a.m. Good night, Kendrick. I love you!

September 16, 1995

Hi Sweetie. Time is going in slow motion. We're not motivated so we're wasting a lot of time. We walked around downtown Rogers a little bit today. I'd always wanted to do that with you and Keegan and then go to lunch at a restaurant downtown. Well, we just walked around. We needed to get out of the house. Sue McLaughlin (neighbor) brought over chili for dinner. Keegan went over to see Jenny (Sue's daughter) and play with the kitties. She wants one and thinks she's going to get one. We went to Kmart this evening, too. I miss you everywhere we go. I watched part of the video Rochelle took when she was in California. That is going to be so precious to have that tape of you. Especially since you are showing your art work and dream homes.

I think I'm getting better with accepting your death. If that's what you call it. I don't like the term accepting. That makes it sound like it's okay and it will never be okay that you are gone. You were my special boy and I love you so. I wanted you here with me forever. I'm always wondering what you're doing in heaven. I need to learn so much.

I look forward to going to church tomorrow. It is so uplifting. I need to be around people. There are so many memories of you around the house that I get sad often. Today I played solitaire on the computer and I pictured you telling me what to do. I always used to tell you not to say anything until I had a chance to figure it out. You were always better than me. I looked at your computer games, too. I was sad you weren't here with me and I cried as I played.

We rented a movie tonight called <u>Nell</u>. It's on now and I'm half watching. Slowly we're moving on with a life without you. I guess we have no choice. After you died I fantasized that you might be a new messiah. After all, you were a great child and maybe you could come back to life. But, you're really gone and we'll have to wait to see you when we come to join you. Until then, we're going to do our best to keep your memory alive and to make a difference in this world where we can.

When I read these notes, I realize how I grasped at any straw I could. I just wanted Kendrick to be alive. I kept expecting him to come back and anything that could possibly make that happen, including being sent from God, was fair game. I would replay everything in my mind and wonder what a different outcome may have been if we had made any different choices in our life. Would Kendrick have died if we had still been in California? He wanted to play football, so he would have been playing at a different school. Would Kendrick have survived if I hadn't gone to Atlanta? Would Kendrick have survived if we had bought a different house? The EMT's had a hard time getting him out from the downstairs, and maybe a one-level house or a house closer to school would have been better. Yes, I know, only God knows the number of our days, but as grieving parents we still ask why and try to change the outcome.

> *I know that Dad and I are strong people. We have been tested and strengthened over the years and now we've faced the ultimate test. Why do we have to be tested like this? What is the purpose of your death? You were so perfect even on earth. My sweet child, I miss you so.*

By now you probably are wondering why I keep talking about Kendrick being so perfect. Did he do everything right? Uh, no, he was a typical child. But when a child dies, it is normal for a parent to put the child on a pedestal. Typically, the good memories remain and the unpleasant fade. Kendrick was a very good child and we even had parents tell us they were glad that their child was Kendrick's friend because he was such a good example. We went to teacher conferences and loved to hear how nice a child he was. So, forgive me for only telling you the wonderful. He was perfection in my mind and the fact that I couldn't get him to wash his hair, walk faster, pick up his dirty clothes, or do his homework does not in the least matter!

September 17, 1995

Hi Honey. Today was pretty good, but it seems like you've been gone so long. It almost seems like you've been gone forever. Does that mean I'm getting used to not having you here? It doesn't do any good to be angry or sad, but I am. I talk myself out of it most of the time. I just remember how lucky I was to have you as my son, and that I get to be with you in eternity. I'm trying not to be selfish and cry about what I'm missing out with you gone, because you lived 13 ½ happy years on earth. You always seemed to have wisdom beyond your years. Were you just here for a purpose and your purpose was done? Or is your purpose going to be served through your death?

We went to church this morning. I didn't like when they mentioned football or when the school superintendent spoke—those things contributed to your death.

We met with another lawyer this afternoon. He seems very experienced. It is hard to know what to do.

Jenny McLaughlin brought home some of your artwork from school. It was nice to get. I wish we would have saved more of your stuff. I hope I find more around here. Jenny had told her mom that she thought you were so cute and all the girls did. I always knew you were so handsome, but you were beautiful on the inside, too, and that's what made you a beautiful person.

I didn't cry today. I think it's the first day since your accident that I didn't. It feels strange, though. I still have the ache of missing you like there is a wrench tightening my stomach and, if released, I would just fly off like a balloon.

I have read many books on death and angels and grief over these weeks. They have helped a lot. Maybe that is why I'm recovering or at least I feel like I'm recovering. It is good to recover because we have so much to do to amend this wrong to some extent. You should be here with us. We should get to see you grow up and we should get to hold your children and I should have gotten to hear many more "Good night, Mom, I love you's."

I bought you those comic books you wanted when I left Atlanta the day of your accident. I was hoping you'd be able to read them soon. You have quite a few that you never recovered to read. I was so anxious for your recovery to give you all your heart's desire. But, I guess heaven is a wonderful place and I'm sure any earthly pleasures would not begin to compare with the joys you are experiencing in heaven.

I'm back at work tomorrow. The future seems irrelevant without you, but you know we're not quitters. We just feel like it—or I do. Your Dad never does. He's a fighter like you. We have so much to accomplish to keep your memory alive, make a difference for a better earthly world, and build our treasures in heaven. We already have one of our greatest treasures in heaven.

Good night, Kendrick. I love you. My heart is broken.

September 18, 1995

Hi Honey. I had a tough day at work today. It was hard to think about work. But I was physically there for eight hours—which was a big step. I even sat through a 1 ½ hour meeting. I had to shut my door and cry a little this morning. I called Daddy and he'd just finished being sad so he could listen to me and be sad.

People just don't know what to say to me so they are avoiding me or just not talking to me. That makes me feel bad. I feel so lonesome for you anyhow and I'd like people to talk to.

We have a bunch of thank you notes to write. Lots of people sent us sympathy cards. It is so sad and I am glad people care enough to send a card. Some have sent nice letters too. And some people I would have liked to hear from, I haven't. You have taught us so much about death and now we can help others. I've been having trouble sleeping, but I guess that is normal for grief.

Some people do not know how to handle grieving friends. There is one particular close friend that I never heard from after Kendrick died. After about a month I called her and said, "You know Kendrick died?" She said she did but she didn't know what to say so she hadn't called. I don't know if we ever talked again. I was a changed person. She couldn't deal with a friend that lost a child.

Understand that your friend is grieving, too. They are not grieving the loss of their child, but they are grieving that their friend is hurting and they may also be grieving for your child if they were close. It is helpful to be understanding and give them time to get to know the new person that you are becoming.

Keegan is sure getting a lot more attention. You'd be so jealous. But, you know, when I was with you in the hospital, I was thinking about all the things I would do with you when you got out. We had to go school shopping, and I was going to spoil you rotten at Christmas. I was looking forward to taking you out to all your favorite places to eat. I'm glad we ate at Ryan's the night before your accident because that was your favorite restaurant. Daddy made you promises, too. Aunty Sheryl said she was keeping a list for you to make sure we didn't renege on any of them.

Keegan and I went on a frog hunt this evening. We found a brownish frog so she can bring it to school tomorrow. They are having a unit on frogs.

You know, sometimes when I'm writing, I really feel like you will be reading this. Just like when I'm doing things I think, "I can't wait to tell Kendrick." Or, when I'm looking at cards I think, "Kendrick will be so pleased when he sees all these." Kind of strange—the reason I'm writing this and the reason for the cards is because you're gone. When we were getting goodie baskets at the hospital I was anxious for you to get well so you could enjoy them. Then when we got home and everyone started bringing by food we were sad because you would have enjoyed all the food. We couldn't enjoy it because the reason it was here was because you weren't. There is such irony in this life.

Well Sweetie, I'm going to get to sleep if possible. I'm tired, but that doesn't mean much lately.

I love you. This pain in my stomach and the panic in my heart are still here. Good night, Kendrick. I love you.

September 19, 1995

Hi Honey. Today is Grandma Roseland's birthday. I called her to wish her a happy birthday. She is very sad and still very angry. I told her she needs to let go of that anger—"God grant me the serenity to accept the things I cannot change, courage to change the things I can, and the wisdom to know the difference." I bought her a little card that has that on it to send her.

This is so very hard. I had a meeting at work this morning. I made it through a half hour of business and then I ended up starting to cry. So everybody left and Darell Floyd stayed to talk to me. I still have a hard time fathoming that you aren't coming back. I don't like that I don't get to see you grow up.

I just got a call from Colleen Cadreau (friend from Minnesota*). She and Sandy Greene* (friend from Minnesota) *are going to come visit in a week and a half. That will be nice. I'll have to think of some activity they will enjoy.*

I am so sad you're not here. I get cranky at Dad. I hope he is okay. He's been sleeping a lot and started watching television. You were his best buddy here and he's so alone. I'm able to go to work and Keegan to school. Think I'll go to sleep. I'm really tired again. Just hope I can sleep. I miss you so Honey--I love you, good night.

Chapter 3

Life Is Pulling Me Forward

Life is pulling me forward not because I want it to, but because that is life.

September 20, 1995 - Wednesday

Hi Kendrick. Life is moving on. I wonder how your life is. We met Aileah today. She is a nice girl. I don't know why you never told us about her. Yes, Daddy would have teased you mercilessly, but I wouldn't have. I did always tell you that you were my baby, though, and too young to like girls. We gave her the t-shirt from Little Rock and a plant. We knew you'd want her to have something. She wrote a poem for you, too. You were really special to her.

I met with a counselor tonight. She says my grief process is "normal" because not everyone grieves the same way. Each person chooses their own path of grieving. I just want to make sure I'm working through the grief and not around it.

We looked at the video from California that Aunt Shelly (this is my sister Rochelle, we frequently referred to her as Aunt Shelly) took again tonight when Aileah was here. It made me sad because

I still have a hard time believing you will never be here on earth again. We have so many years of sorrow ahead of us.

Today I was imagining you telling me, "Make a difference, Mom." I want that to be my motto. This is a time for us of reevaluating our goals and priorities and what we want out of life and what we want to do for others. Material things are no longer important. We want to build up the treasures in heaven. I'm thinking about checking out the theology or sociology doctorate programs at the university. I've been interested in that for a while but I have a good job and that seemed frivolous and selfish. Now, those interests could help us strive to make a difference.

Keegan still sleeps on your pillow. We haven't washed the pillowcase yet. It still smells like you. I remember when I always used to tell you to keep your greasy hair off the couch pillows. Now, I smell them to see if I can catch a scent of you.

It is still so overwhelmingly unreal that this has happened. God is being good to us and blessing us with strength. I need to begin getting my focus on work, too. I feel very distracted at work and it is hard to concentrate.

Well, I better go to sleep. I blew you a kiss. Good night, Kendrick. I love you.

September 21, 1995

I didn't want to get up this morning. Sometimes facing another day without you is just too challenging. Fear paralyzes me. I still don't believe that you can be gone. I have so much love to give you yet and you're not here to receive it. I haven't had enough time to read this week now that I am back at work. I find comfort in reading to help understand death and grieving.

*My former managers from Chicago and San Leandro called today.
I can transfer to either of those places if I want. It's hard to know
what to do, but for now, this is home. Your memories are here. You
loved Rogers and wanted to stay here. We have to ensure justice is
served before we move on. I'd like it if we could stay.*

I worked for a great company and had a great job. But just as with
friends, employers constitute people who do not always know how to
deal with grief. A company's ultimate concern is their performance.
Some companies have programs that assist people with grief and other
life issues, but it really is your responsibility to take charge of your grief
and ensure you can move forward. Take advantage of your friends,
services available from your employer, your church, and other avenues;
but make sure you are giving your job as much as you can, because
they have hired you to perform a job. Most employers will understand
for a time, but that time expires very quickly in the mind of a grieving
parent.

Kendrick's death was prominently in the news and I believe was one of
the factors that led them to ask me to relocate. In June, I had actually
asked my manager if I could be transferred because I didn't think
this location was a good fit for me. I was denied that transfer request
because I had not been here long enough. In July, corporate decided
that I should report to a manager in Atlanta instead of the manager in
Chicago that I had been reporting to. After Kendrick died, the pressure
started immediately to move to another location. My manager came to
my house after the funeral and asked where I would like to live. After
Kendrick died the last thing on my mind was packing up his room and
moving.

*We want to build your baseball park. There are so many wonderful
people in this town, so if we can find comfort here it may be the
place we need to stay. I often wonder if this would have happened*

34

had we stayed in California. I can only believe that this must have all been in God's plan for our lives. You know, I often thought you were so special. One time when you were about nine years old I remember you crying and saying you didn't want to die. I remember thinking about God taking the really special children and I hoped that you weren't too special to stay with us.

Grandpa Fincher is even starting to go to church. I guess maybe you had to go first to help pave the way for those of us who were wandering. Even though our prayers for you to be healed here on earth were not part of God's plan, we have been drawn to the religious community. I know church doesn't get a person to heaven but it helps to keep us guided on the right path.

Daddy is watching too much TV. You know how much I hate TV and wasting that time. So, I get angry. I'd like him to get ambitious again, but I know it must be hard for him. He's here all alone during the day and I know I can't tolerate the loneliness.

Please keep your spirit comforting us. I worry about Keegan, too. I'm not sure she understands that she will never see you again on earth. She draws pictures for you. I think she's denying you are gone. Grandma and Grandpa Roseland and Grandpa Fincher are so sad, too, and very angry. They need so much comfort and they need to let go of the anger. We need to feel your loving spirit around us and comforting us.

I think when I die I want to know I'm dying. I want a chance to say goodbye and talk to all the people I love and care about. You know, they never really said you could survive. They kept telling us how sick you were, but I never believed you would die. I had so much faith that God would help you get well. Every time they told us you were failing, and even when they didn't, your life was *always tenuous in the hospital. I had this pain in my stomach and heart and a weakness in my legs, but I always believed you would be a miracle. Until that last night that Dad called.*

For me, this is one of the hardest parts of my memories. This is when all hope was lost and I knew it was time.

Grandma and I had just gone to bed at Ronald McDonald's House at midnight. I remember Grandma putting on her pajamas and I was thinking I didn't want to because I wanted to be able to get up quickly if need be. At 1 a.m. Dad called and said, "I think you better come over," and I felt a sense of dread.

Grandma and I shot out of bed and said, "Oh, God, no," and we were each praying our own frantic prayers out loud. As we walked to the hospital we clasped arms. I started singing "How Great thou Art." When did your spirit leave your body? When we got to the room you were bleeding from somewhere. They were giving you fluids, plasma, blood and platelets to help keep your blood pressure up but you were doing extremely poorly. Blood was coming out of your mouth. Daddy and I took turns suctioning out the blood so it didn't run down your face. It was horrible to feel you were dying but yet praying and hoping to God that there would be a miracle. At 7 a.m. they decided to do an EEG to check your brain function. They thought seizures may have caused more damage and they thought you may still be having seizures. Then they kicked us out at 7:30 as your life signs started dropping. I could tell by the look on their faces it was not good. We went to the chapel to wait. At 9:45 a.m. the chaplain came in to get us. We knew, or at least I did, that it must be time to say goodbye. Our nightmare . . . can this be real?

The doctor told us right away, "He's going to die." I asked the doctor some questions that I don't even remember and then realized we needed to say goodbye. It, as I look back, was strange. I so gracefully accepted the fact that I needed to say goodbye to you. How could I do that? How could I say goodbye to my only precious son without wailing and screaming and refusing to accept your death, but I did. I told you goodbye. Did you hear us? Was your spirit still there? Or were the machines just keeping your body functioning and warm?

You were so beautiful. It was so hard to watch you struggle for 18 days, but it would have all been worth it to have you here. Maybe I am being selfish to want you here with me. After all, heaven is great isn't it? You lived 13 ½ great years here on earth with people that gave you lots of love. You never have to know the pains of growing up. You were such a great kid. I had no doubt you would grow into an outstanding adult. This life always has challenges and we work through them because we are so tied to this life—and now that you've had a taste of heaven you would not want to trade for this world, would you? A mother is always supposed to want what's best for her son. Are you in the best place for you now? God has healed you, you just aren't here with us.

Good night Kendrick. I love you, forever.

September 22, 1995

Hi Sweetie. Today was a pretty good day for me. Dad had a rough day. I came home for lunch and I'm glad I did because we were able to talk and I think he felt better when I went back to work. I think I'm in denial today. I can't believe you're not coming back. Every day when I drop off Keegan I think I should be dropping off you, too. I know what I would be saying: "Hurry up, are you ready to get out?" If you had made me run late I'd suggest you walk from the corner, but, of course, I'd never make you do that. You'd look at me with that half grin "ah, Mom" look and I'd just laugh and drop you off at the door.

Of course, I wouldn't get a kiss in front of school, but I'd try sneak one before we got to school. I'd say "Bye, Kendrick, have a good day."

You'd say, "Bye, Mom, have a good day." Now, with you gone it's hard to have good days. They are getting a little easier. I'm beginning to smile again, even laugh. I can make it through a day without crying.

A man at work came in to visit with me today. He said something really special—he said he's cried three times in his life that he remembers and two were when his daughters were born and one was when he read in the paper that you died. You've touched a lot of hearts. We're going to keep on fighting for you, Baby, and keep on touching lives. You were much too special to let your sensitivity and compassion die, too.

It is hard to know how we'll find the strength to do what we need to do. But I know it will come. Our purpose is you--the child that we mourn for and cherish and the memories of you, the handsome blond son that I was watching grow up and that I wanted to have around me forever. I even knew you'd take care of me when I got old because you were so caring.

Aunt Sheryl comes tomorrow and will be here till next Thursday. That will be good for Dad. Keegan will be excited to have her here but I bet she won't want to go to school.

God bless your soul. You had such a beautiful soul even here on earth. I pray that God is rewarding you for all the joy you brought into our lives and for being such a great son. Love you, Honey— good night.

September 23, 1995

Oh, Saturday—a day when we all would have been home together. We would have picked out a movie at Blockbusters and watched it tonight. Dad and you would be lying on the floor in the bedroom and Keegan and I in the bed. I would have told you not to get your greasy hair on the pillow shams. I remember I always told you keep your greasy hair off the pillows and then after we came home after you'd died I picked up the pillows and tried to smell your scent.

Life is painful. I try to keep busy and have people around me and that helps. I don't know though if that's just avoiding my grief or helping me get through it.

Grandpa Fincher called this evening. He's worried about Keegan. I am too. I just don't know if she's dealing with your death or denying it. Grandpa said his dad died when he was eight. He said he built a wall around himself because he didn't want to get hurt again and he's just now, after your death, allowing that wall to come down. He said even his own family members don't really know him. You were very special to Grandpa and this is very hard on him, too. There were so many people that were proud to know you. And many people now that wish they knew you better or at all because of what they have heard about you. What a wonderful memory to leave my dear son.

How fortunate I was to have you. I wish I could have had you with me all my living days but I know one day God will be able to make this all clear. You will be able to tell me, too, with your new wisdom.

I feel comforted most of the time. I focus on how blessed I was to have you. Had God given me a choice to have you for 13 ½ years or not at all, I would have taken the 13 ½ years. You taught us a lot when you were on earth and you are teaching us through your death.

I worry about us filing a lawsuit. I don't want people to misunderstand. We are angry, we want justice, and we want your memory to be kept alive and visible. This was not supposed to happen to you—or was it? Was this an accident or was it God's plan? I sure have a lot of questions for you and God.

I see your smiling face on the photos around the house. What a happy boy you were. You were so happy to be alive and so joyful over the simple pleasures in life. It never took much to make you happy. We never had to spend lots of money. You were ecstatic over a trip to McDonalds or just some extra attention. I remember how proud you were when I took vacation days to go with you on your field trips. Remember the time we did the teepee and when we went on the prairie? Those were really special. You were also so proud when Daddy helped at your track and field day at school. On Thursday Keegan and I went to her open house at school. I remembered how proud you were at your open houses showing me around and sharing your school work with me. Your teachers always told me what a good kid you were and I always said, "I know, he's a really good kid." We took so much pride in seeing such a nice young man be our son. Yes, you were our son and you were loved by many and respected by friends and their parents alike. It seems like we were doing a good job as parents so why did you have to go? I know you will never know the sorrows of this world. You will not have the joys of this world either, but God says the joys of heaven are so much better. I guess you get the best of both worlds!

My beloved son, I pray that God will guide us. Good night, Kendrick. I love you.

September 24, 1995

Sunday . . . each day the intense pain gets softer and the loneliness for you grows stronger. My child who always had a laugh or a joke, your absence is felt strongly. I was pretty much into self-pity today. It seems like the world should just stop and wait till I'm okay, but then again, will I ever be okay?

I'm getting cranky at Dad a lot. You know how I always used to hate his pokiness—well, now, it aggravates me even more. He takes so long to get around to doing something and he is always late. If I tell him 4:00, he's ready at 5:00. I should focus more on his good qualities. He's a good father and he never complains. He does a lot around the house that most men would never do. I wish that he had more ambition but I guess ambition is more than just a pristine yard and house and he has ambition in his heart. I need to learn patience more.

Back to work tomorrow. It's going to be a busy week at work and home. But, I guess I won't have too much time for contemplation. I feel like I have so much to do though. I should be more like you and just do what's important at the time and not worry too much about stuff that's really not important in the scheme of things.

I would like to have a week or two to just read. There is so much I want to learn. We copied all the newspaper articles today so we can send them to those that asked for copies.

Tomorrow we get to go to your memorial at St. Mary's Hospital. These past seven weeks have been a horrible nightmare. Too bad I can't wake up from it and have you here with us. Life is so unfair—or is it fair—was it "fair" for you to be taken and we just don't know that? Good night, Kendrick. I love you.

September 25, 1995

Hi Honey. We went to the memorial service at St. Mary's this evening. It was for all the people that lost a loved one recently. Aunt Sheryl went with us, too. Brother Stephen and Sister Concepta were there. They were with Dad the day you were brought into the hospital. They both commented how senseless your death was and expressed anger at the coaches. Sister Concepta said you have touched a lot of lives. She said one of the doctors who went to your funeral cancelled a meeting that afternoon and went home to be with her kids.

It was hard for Dad to go to the hospital tonight because of the bad memories of the day you got sick. I think it was a little healing though. You really had a wonderful dad. He has such a kind heart. I don't know why he has always had such tough breaks.

Work passed slowly today, but I did get some productive work done. So much of what I do has been "busy work." I'm starting to try to focus on what's really important at work so I can spend more time focusing on what is really important—family!

Colleen and Sandy will be here this weekend. I'm really looking forward to them being here--someone new to listen to me. Some people are such good listeners.

The past couple of days I have been looking at my blessings. I really shouldn't feel too blessed because you are gone, but I'm taking a look at what I do have—and I have so much to be thankful for. I'm sure God has blessings intended to come out of your death. I would never imagine blessings from a senseless death, but we are to give thanks in everything. And, I guess, my thanks is that I was so blessed to have you. I'm blessed to have such great memories.

We're going to finish watching the videos on angels. Good night, Honey.

September 26, 1995

Today was a day that was beginning to feel "normal." I know we need to develop a new "normal" in our lives. Daddy and I went to meet with friends tonight and we were able to visit in the car. I told him how I'm feeling like the guilt and most of the anger has passed and I am sad you are gone and I miss you a lot, but, I feel okay—like maybe this is acceptance. He said he feels the same. We saw a shack on the way out to their house and I said I'd be so happy living there if only I could have you back again. We talked about what we need to do in our life for you. You're our inspiration. It seems like you've been gone so long. It seems like we're getting "used to" you being gone . . . that is so awful to feel that way because that is something I never dreamed I'd have to do. Then sometimes I look at your photo and I can't believe you're gone . . . sometimes I look at your photo and can't believe I ever had you. What is a dream and what is reality? It is so easy to be confused. I don't cry much anymore. I feel like I have a shell around me and I'm stoic. Mundane day-to-day trivialities are starting to get my attention again, but I am changed. My life is changed--all because I had this wonderful son for 13 years. How lucky I was. God truly blessed me by letting you be a part of my life. I can't wait to see you in heaven. I love you, Kendrick.

Every once in a while I drive by the shack that we saw on that drive. However, this shack has since been remodeled and looks like a very nice, well-cared for home. I am reminded that with love and care, everything can be new again--even our lives. My life was a shambles back in 1995 and, just like the house that looks like a home, my life is good again. I don't have Kendrick, but I have lots of love in my life and lots to be thankful for. I will always miss Kendrick and wish he were here, but I can still have a good life.

September 27, 1995

Some days it seems like you have been gone for so long. I met with the counselor tonight. She thinks I'm doing "okay" and said I should just call her when I feel a need to make an appointment.

I just noticed on this photo I'm looking at of Keegan next to one of yours that her hands look a lot like yours. I always loved your hands. Remember I always held your hand when you were little and then as you got older we held hands sometimes when we watched TV or when we were in the car. Then in the hospital I held your hand most of the time I was in your room. In the first few days when they didn't give us much hope for your survival I would rub each finger over and over and keep repeating "God bless Kendrick and make him well." That was a count of seven words and I always thought seven was my lucky number, too. I guess God did bless you and make you well—only you're with him and not with me. That is not exactly like I had envisioned.

I am totally amazing myself with the strength I have been given to go on with life. I keep wondering how I'm doing this day-to-day life and actually functioning very well, I think, considering your death. I believe God and your spirit are strengthening me. There is so much to do. Good night, Kendrick. I love you! I love you! I love you!

September 28, 1995

I would call today a bad day. You're gone and that's bad enough. My stomach is in a knot. I need to cry and I can't. I think I am angry at pretty much everything and everyone.

I'm really mad at Dad. I don't even know if I love him. He can be such a nice person and then he can be so stupid, inconsiderate, and insensitive. When you were here I tolerated him more because our family was so important. Now, I don't know what's important. I don't think anything is except Keegan now.

The news station stopped over today. Dad didn't say much to them, though. They filmed him and he didn't know it. Dad let them take a couple shots of your picture and the family picture Christine (cousin) had taken in California.

I've been able to do okay at night because I just read until I am falling asleep. In the morning I dread another day without you.

There's a football game tomorrow night. You should have been playing. I was so looking forward to going to the games and watching you play. Keegan's brushing my hair. The other day when she was combing Dad's hair she combed it like you combed yours. You looked so much like Dad.

I am so unhappy. I don't know what to do. I guess I know what I should do, but I don't want to do anything. I just want to lie down and cry myself to sleep, but I can't even cry. I think I am so mad.

Well, I just had to stop writing and cry a little. It still doesn't feel better though. I guess I better start exercising like the counselor said. That will maybe help my anger.

Back to reading until I can't keep my eyes open. Tomorrow Friday—five weeks since you died. I thought I was doing pretty well—I've got a long way to go. Good night, Kendrick—I love you.

September 29, 1995

Hi Honey. Today was sure an up and down day. I woke up early this morning and just lay awake in bed until the alarm went off. I don't like facing a new day without you. I remember Jim Olson (friend from Colorado, his wife Olivia watched Keegan from 3 weeks old until we moved to California when Keegan was 4) *told me, "Rhonda, any day is a good day when you wake up and you're alive." I think that I should add, "and you have those you love alive with you." Good days are hard to come by lately.*

Patty Larson (friend from Colorado) *called me this morning. It was nice to visit with her. We chatted and cried for quite awhile.*

Sandy and Colleen arrived about 9:00 tonight. It sure is nice to have them here. I even laughed lots with them—just like old times. We're going to go to flea markets tomorrow.

Keegan stayed at Jenny's tonight and tomorrow she is going to a computer class. Grandpa Fincher and Grandma Roseland both think she may be using Jenny to kind of take the place of the fun she had with you.

It's really late (1:15 a.m.) and I feel more wound up than tired. I suppose I won't sleep too late tomorrow since Sandy and Colleen are here. I miss you so much. There are so many memories of you and I still think of you almost constantly. Life is so very strange—I still feel like this is a dream. I LOVE YOU!!

September 30, 1995

Sandy, Colleen and I took Shadow (our dog) *for a walk this morning. You should have been here for our trek today, but had you not died, they probably wouldn't have come. This afternoon we drove over to Eureka Springs and stopped at a bunch of flea markets along the way. Sandy got car sick and she was throwing up in downtown Eureka Springs.*

Colleen and I looked at photos this evening. We have so many wonderful memories. You were a one-of-a-kind son—we were so lucky to have you. How I wish you could have stayed with us. In everything I do I sense emptiness in my heart.

Your sister is sleeping with your baseball shirt tonight. She had to get a pumpkin for Brother today too. She remembers when the two of you carved pumpkins last year. She doesn't have her older brother to go trick or treating with this year.

I found a penny this morning on the walk so I told Sandy and Colleen my penny story. Good night, Kendrick. I love you!!!!!!!!!!!

And, readers, you get to hear my penny story, too! When Kendrick was in the hospital, the day before he died I found a few pennies . . . on the floor in the waiting room, at the pay phone cubicle where I went to call people, in the hallway. When we got home from the hospital after he died and I opened my suitcase, pennies fell out. Maybe I had put the pennies in my pocket and they had fallen out. I don't know, but it all seemed very strange. Then as months went by, I kept finding pennies in the most comforting places . . . the floor of the prosecutor's office, the way in to the hospital for the memorial service, in New York City with the year of Kendrick's birth on the penny. It seemed like I would always find a penny at the perfect time to give me comfort. To this day, I still pick up pennies, frequently look at the date, and save them all in my "pennies from heaven" jar.

October 1, 1995

Kendrick . . . I really love that name. We have to make sure there are a lot of memories that go on forever with that name. I wonder if your name is Kendrick in heaven.

Colleen, Sandy, Keegan and I went to flea markets again today. I missed having you with us. I looked at a couple comic books and wondered if they were ones you'd want to buy. It is hard to fully comprehend you will not be back to share anything with us here on earth.

It is good we have been through so much change in our lives over the past years. I think that is helping us cope with the sadness (change) of having you gone. We've learned to let go of the past and move on to the future no matter how bleak or unknown it appears.

I survive on the wonderful memories of you. Life is so hard but I think of your smiles and I remember you would laugh at me when I'd worry too much. There is a Compassionate Friends meeting tomorrow night. I'm not sure if I'll go or not. Dad says he doesn't want to go.

I dislike when I hear about football at Elmwood (the school Kendrick was attending). *You should have been alive and I would have gone and watched you play. Now, there shouldn't even be football this year. You died and their lives are continuing like nothing happened. I pray that God will take vengeance because "vengeance is mine saith the Lord."*

Wow, I read some of what I wrote and I cringe. I am trying to stay true to my feelings at the time and not edit away what might be controversial or embarrassing now. I was very angry. I wanted someone to take responsibility. I wanted everyone else to feel as bad as I did. I have forgiven all concerned with Kendrick's death, including myself. What? Yes, including myself. You see, if I had checked out what football practice consisted of in Arkansas back in 1995, Kendrick may have survived. If his Dad knew the signs and symptoms of heat illness, he would have taken Kendrick to the hospital immediately and Kendrick may have survived. The coaches were doing what they thought their job was and we have worked to educate coaches on heat illness prevention through the Kendrick Fincher Memorial Foundation (see end of book for more details on the Foundation).

People may be surprised when they don't hear me talking bad about coaches. I think coaches are some of the most underappreciated people in the world. Many of them are paid very little for their extra or volunteer assignments. I don't believe any of them go in to coaching to make children miserable or to have them die. They coach because they love sports, they want to instill the love of sports in children, and some of the great ones desire to be a positive influence in the lives of children. Some coaches need more training in appropriate conditioning and heat illness prevention and, I believe, that was the case the day Kendrick experienced heat stroke.

> *Well, I'm going to try get some sleep and hope I don't wake up too early in the morning because I just lie there and think of you and that is fearsome each morning. Good night, Kendrick—I love you.*

> *October 2, 1995*

> *I feel such a great emptiness this morning. I woke up at 4 a.m. and Sandy and Colleen had already left. Then I went to the couch and kneeled like I had the night before your accident. I could picture you lying on the couch and me talking to you and holding your hand. It is so hard to believe I will not hold that hand again. I cried and*

I prayed. Kendrick, you mean so much to me. Your absence is so great.

I went to the dentist today. I wondered if you had sat in that chair and looked out the window at the dentist's office the week before the accident when you had your teeth cleaned. I remember you were so proud because, once again, you didn't have any cavities.

We had a quiet evening tonight. It's the first free evening we've had in over a week, but now it makes me lonely. It's better when we are busy. We still have lots of thank you notes to do so that will occupy our evenings. We watched some TV tonight. That was very strange because you liked TV so much and you weren't here with us. Now we're such zombies we can't do much else. We also got two $25,000 checks for your life insurance today. Both Dad and I cried. I said I'd like to pay the coach $50,000 for a glass of water and have you back here with me. The money is just going in the savings account until we know if we'll get a ball park.

We were fortunate to have good medical insurance through work and an insurance policy that covered funeral expenses. When Kendrick was young we took out a college savings/life insurance plan that would mature when he was 18. Little did we think we would be using the life insurance portion of the plan. For us, there was never any consideration of using the $50,000 for anything personal. How could you go on a vacation or buy a car or anything else with money from your child's death? The money eventually went to establish the Kendrick Fincher Memorial Foundation.

Life seems to be getting more painful. Your absence is becoming more final. Today was eight weeks since your accident. It seems like a lifetime ago. I thought about going to Compassionate Friends this evening but Kathy Ives (friend from Colorado) *called and we ended up visiting too long. She just got my letter today so she was pretty shook up.*

I've been so worthless at work. I have to get motivated!

It's after 11 p.m. and Keegan isn't asleep yet. She'll be hard to get up in the morning. I probably will be, too.

Well, Sweetie, my love for you continues to grow . . . one day closer to heaven. Good night, Kendrick. I love you!

October 3, 1995

I got to talk to a couple people at work about you today. I like to talk about you even though it is sad. I like people to hear what really happened. Our lawyers sound like they are being careful and thorough. The prosecutor's office is talking to the kids this week. I pray the truth will be found and people will help us ensure it doesn't happen again. I also hope there are criminal charges so a precedent is set and other coaches think twice before they use life-threatening conditioning practices.

I miss you so very much. Keegan is sitting next to me whining—you were so different. I miss asking you if your homework is done and if you're ready to go and if you've got your shoes on. I miss saying, "Kendrick and Keegan, dinner is ready." Now I just say, "Dinner's ready." We don't all sit down much together anymore for meals. I'm sure we'll get back to some normalcy at some point. We are going through quite an adjustment now. For some reason I am very tired tonight. It is only 10:00 and I'm going to try sleep. Good night, Kendrick . . . I love you.

October 4, 1995

Kendrick . . . I so love that name. If only I could turn back the clock of time to August 6th or even the morning of August 7th. Who would ever think you would die from football practice? I miss you so much. On my way home from work tonight I was thinking about how I used to hold your hand or put my hand on your knee and pat your knee when I was driving. I always liked having you close.

I wrote on some thank you notes tonight. I will be sad when I'm done because these are the last cards I will sign "Kendrick Fincher," even though the words before them are "the family of."

I think of how much you were enjoying life. You had so many dreams and goals. You designed so many dream homes. I feel like I'm starting over a new life. All I have ever lived for is totally changed. All my future is changed. I will always mourn that I don't have you here with me. I have such a great emptiness that will always be felt in my heart, soul and mind. My one-of-a-kind, special, loving son has gone to be with the loving Father in heaven. My only comfort is that you are in heaven, safe, happy, and that I will be with you again one day. What will that be like? Will you have grown older and I'll have missed seeing you mature? Will you still be my son? Or, was my turn as having you as my son done when you died—do you now belong only to God? I have so many questions and no one to answer them.

Keegan got a little black kitty from Jennifer today. She's trying to think of a special name for it. She's sleeping with it right now. Keegan has been sleeping with or wearing your Mariners t-shirt (this is the baseball shirt from Kendrick's team the summer before he died). *Today she also brought it with her to school. She really misses you. We all do.*

Aunty Shelly is feeling really down. She's fearful of her cancer and her fate. She's got her three kids here so she wants to live. I pray that she will live for many, many years to see her kids grow up and marry and have grandkids. She needs strength and God's blessings, though. What do you think? Do you know what's going to happen to her?

In March 1995, my sister Rochelle was diagnosed with stage 4 breast cancer. Her children were only 5, 3 and 1 when she was diagnosed with cancer. That was a hard time for my family as we went through the shock of possibly losing someone so dear to us. We were all concerned with Rochelle and her cancer and then Kendrick died unexpectedly five months later. Life can play some strange tricks on a person.

Well, I'm getting sleepy and as the week wears on it's harder to get up in the mornings. Tomorrow is Thursday. I'm looking forward to this weekend so I can get a bunch of stuff done around the house. The weekends are sometimes hard because we always did family activities. Good night, Kendrick . . . I love you!!!!!

October 5, 1995 - Thursday

Today Aileah came over. She is going to draw a picture of the four of us from photos. Jenny was over quite a bit this afternoon too. She liked playing Yukon Trail and Kids Sing Along with Keegan. She had dinner with us too. That was nice to have her over. She's going to babysit Keegan tomorrow night.

We got some information on heat stroke from the lawyer today. Pretty much everything was wrong at practice to contribute to your heat stroke. It's almost like you were being set up for heat stroke. There were so many factors contributing to make your condition deadly. Dad read a list of factors that can contribute and you had all the factors.

Jenny was telling us about the kids that we thought were good kids and they are actually not very good. We really were lucky with you. Jenny said you really were a good kid at school, too. She said everyone thought you were real sweet. Kindness is always good isn't it?

I'm getting crabby again because I'm angry you're gone. There should be so much that we'd be doing together. I wish I would have saved more of your things like clothes, artwork, etc., because now we don't get to create any more memories with you and the ones we have need to last a lifetime. Good night, Kendrick—I love you.

October 6, 1995 - Friday

The weeks are sure long. I think it's been five weeks since you died. It seems so long. I miss you so much now and I miss you more each day. No wonder people say it gets harder. It is hard to believe there are so many other parents who have lost children and they go on to "live" their lives. I bet they are always in pain and always feel emptiness.

Today at work someone said something teasingly to me about someone else picking on them, and I said, "Wow it seems like a long time since I've heard something like that." I told her how you and Keegan used to pick on each other and yell, "Mom" and state your complaint. No wonder it is so quiet around here.

Jenny babysat Keegan tonight and they went to the Rogers' High School Homecoming game. Afterwards I walked over to Jenny's to pick up Keegan and I looked up at the stars and I said the wishing upon a star poem—but there is only one wish I want right now and that is for you to be here with us. Your memories are here, but I miss you so much. Kendrick, you were such a wonderful son. I just don't understand why you had to be taken. I hope I can see some positive come out of this pain. I don't know what positive can possibly justify your death but maybe it can help us cope.

I'm glad it is the weekend. I have lots of stuff I'd like to get done around the house. Next weekend we'll be in Denver. It would have been more enjoyable if you were still here. You were always making jokes with Dad. I wonder what families that lose children have in common? Are the kids good or are the parents bad? Do we not love enough or do we love too much? Are you just too special for earth? I just pray that there is a life that is wonderful in heaven and that I will get to spend eternity with you.

Good night, Kendrick . . . I love you . . . I love you!!

October 7, 1995- Saturday

It's 8:20 p.m. and Dad and Keegan are watching TV. It always used to be the four of us watching a rented movie on Saturday night. I really missed you a lot today. We got your yearbook from Harvest Park (the school Kendrick attended in California) *and a letter from Nancy Roden* (Kendrick's babysitter when he was between the ages of 1 and 3 in Grand Forks, North Dakota). *Memories are almost too painful sometimes. When I went to the grocery store this afternoon I remembered when I met you there this summer after baseball practice and you were tossing your ball up in the air and catching it. Then I drove to where Keegan and I always waited for you after practice. I'd wait in the car and read and watch when you hit and Keegan always got out and watched you from the sidewalk. After practice she always ran over to meet you and then raced with you back to the car and then you always would argue about who got the front seat. If you'd sweated too much I'd always make you sit in the back, though. Today, I got out of the car and walked over to the edge of the field. I wished I could pick you up again.*

I feel so old. Almost 36 and I feel like 13 years of my life has just been swept away.

Keegan is sitting next to me wearing your Mariners t-shirt. She's been sleeping with it every night and bringing it with her to school in her backpack. Jenny came over today and made a bracelet with Keegan and played Yukon Trail, too.

We don't know what we should do with your savings. Your statement came today and you had taken out $20 at the Dallas airport when you and Dad were there. Dad said you were looking for comic books. You are missed so much. I cried lots today. The future is scary because I miss you so and I'm sure I'll miss you more as time goes by. Good night Kendrick—I love you!

October 8, 1995 – Sunday

One thing different is we are going to church. I wonder if God would have blessed us with a long life for you if we'd been faithful followers. Well, anyway, we're looking for a good church. I remember when you were little we went to church at the Lutheran Brethren Church in Grand Forks for awhile. After we moved we didn't go much. I thought about it a lot and you even asked about going. So that's why I wonder about God's purpose in all this—was your death the only event that would bring us back to Him? We had so many other trials—could they have been a message and we just never learned so we needed the ultimate lesson? I'm so sorry if that's the length God had to go to.

We went to a Nazarene church today. We all three liked it. They were very friendly and made us feel very welcome. We have some more to try though. I want to go to a Bible-focused church.

We went to Walmart in Springdale today and wandered aimlessly around. Then we drove around and ended up at Monte Ne Chicken for dinner. The McLaughlins ended up getting there shortly before we left. They are such nice neighbors and have been so helpful with everything.

Dad and I were talking about how our life seems to lack purpose. We just seem to be existing and moving on in life—or life is moving on and we are just watching it happen. We are basically wasting time---but, we can't get used to this life without you. I'm so looking forward to the next life when I can be with you again. I hope all my loved ones will be there and we can all live in peace and love and have God's love protecting us and have the joy of heaven around us.

I often wonder what you are doing. Do you think of us? Do you miss us? Are you able to see us? Is heaven really a great place? Oh . . . so many questions and, once again, no answers. What I do know is that I love you so and I miss you so much my heart aches and I can't believe you are gone. My joy will never be complete until I see you again and all my family is in heaven with me.

Good night, Kendrick . . . I love you.

October 9, 1995 – Monday

Today was another non-productive day. I'm frittering away time because I spend so much time being sad. It is hard to focus on anything. I know I need to get busy and be productive. I feel very sad today and near tears or crying. The sadness is so all-encompassing sometimes that I don't know what to do. My mind cannot comprehend the why's of you not being with me anymore. If only I knew you were happy and okay—I mean really. I know what I want to believe and what God says in the Bible—but I don't really know. I guess that's where faith comes in. So I will have faith that you're in heaven and that you have joy that I can't even imagine. I will believe that you are loved and have contentment unmatched in this world. I will believe you are a chosen child and you are with a God of love and you will be our inspiration to have us follow God.

I started reading your picture Bible to Keegan tonight. I know you read it through completely and I'm really glad. I sure ramble a lot when I write in here. I just wish you were next to me and I were holding your hand.

Good night, Kendrick—I love you!

Chapter 4

Everything Will Be Okay

I started trying to convince myself that God only takes special children and that this must have been his will. I found comfort in my family, friends, and reading.

October 10, 1995 – Tuesday

I really considered not opening this book today. It is so easy sometimes to ease the pain by pretending, by pretending you are at Derrick's house for the night or away at Grandma's. What I did realize as I was reading tonight is that you are just away—I just can't come to you.

Rose Peterson (friend from Minnesota) *called tonight. I hadn't talked to her since, well actually, I called her after you died. She couldn't make it to the funeral and Ryan* (Rose's son) *was going to but couldn't. He was taking it pretty hard. Rose called the <u>Mighty Ducks</u> promotion and asked them to please not cut out the part you were in.*

When we went to Minnesota the summer of 1995 before Kendrick died, we stopped at my friend Rose's house. Ryan and Kendrick had gone to be extras on the set of <u>Mighty</u> <u>Ducks</u> when they were filming in the Minneapolis area.

Well, Son, what words of wisdom do you have for me? You were never one to mope or moan about life. How do I get motivated? What is my purpose for life now? Speak to my heart . . . . Good night, Kendrick – I love you!

October 11, 1995 – Wednesday

Grandma Roseland called tonight. I almost dread talking to her now because she is so down and Rochelle is so depressed. It makes me angry. Here I am talking myself out of depression and thinking positive thoughts and then I talk to them and they are so busy talking themselves into depression. I don't have enough comfort for others. I use every ounce of strength I have comforting myself. Their day-to-day life did not get destroyed like mine. They do not live with the continual reminder that you are absent from the daily routine. So, I get angry that they are not there to comfort me and I feel like I need to comfort them.

Life . . . I'm beginning to think it's much too painful. Where is the joy of living? Not that I even want it now because I like to focus on seeing you in heaven, but why do people fear death? We are born to live and die. In a way, if people are Christians, why do they fear death so and cry and mourn for those who died? Self-pity, right? Yes, because we miss you. But we have to accept, face the facts. We need to do something to focus on what we do have control over. Sounds so easy. No, it sounds so painful to let go of the hurt. When I let go of the hurt does that mean I've forgotten or I don't care? No—I love you forever; your memories and my love for you goes on forever. Good night, Kendrick—I love you. Oh, how sad I am that you are gone. Tomorrow we go to Denver for the weekend. You were supposed to be with us.

October 17, 1995

Hi Kendrick—we thought of you a lot this weekend. I know you would have been with Jonathon Rose (Kendrick's close friend from Colorado) *most of the weekend. It seemed like we were "home." Rogers does not seem like home but maybe it will. We've only been in our house six months. We drove by our house in Littleton and also in Boulder. Our street in Littleton had houses all up the block now. No house behind ours, though, so it would still have the great view. It is much nicer where we are now but I'd take any house if you were there. We drove by the Boulder house, too. That still looks pretty good. We walked around Pearl Street Mall and ate at Old Chicago like we used to. Everything was tinged with emptiness. Dad said he missed teasing you about the girls.*

Kendrick, I still cannot fathom the thought of my life without you. I clipped a phrase off my calendar that said "without hope the heart would break." That is so true, because I have the hope of eternity—actually the promise of eternity which helps me live.

It was so nice to see Olivia and Jim this weekend. They are such kind and positive people. Keegan saw the doctor on Friday and it looks like she has to have surgery. I don't dare tell Grandma because she freaks out. What should I do with Grandma? You always had such good ideas.

Keegan was born with hydrocephalus. She had her first surgery at 3 months, second at 6 months, then another in California at age 5. This was to be her fourth surgery. Our worries were always for Keegan since she had the medical issues. Kendrick was always the healthy child.

I have to get up at 4 a.m. and drive to Tulsa to go to a meeting in Chicago. I just realized this is the first time you will be going on a business trip with me because your spirit is now free. I had been dreading leaving town. Now I feel a little better.

Aunty Shelly has more tests this week. I pray they will find what they should, but I pray there's nothing to find. That will help Grandma's and Rochelle's spirits if she is cancer free.

You were such a joy in my life and I miss you so in all I do. The fear, sorrow, and sometimes anger encompass me and I panic. My child, my wonderful child, why does God allow such sorrow? Good night, Kendrick. I love you.

October 19, 1995 – Thursday

Hi Kendrick. I miss you so much. I am very angry today. It is becoming more real that you are gone and I still want to fight to have you here. You were on the news last night and in the newspapers the last two days. The school district came up with new guidelines. That is good but it didn't bring me any peace, because it's not bringing you back. I just pray that God will return soon so I can be with you and we can all be together.

I am cranky, tired, worn out and sad. I don't have much motivation. I'm still wasting so much time.

Dad has pneumonia. The doctor said it's the worst he has seen in anyone the past couple of months. He got medicine and two shots on the butt—he said you'd be laughing! His fever is still 102. It was 103 last night. He's getting lots of rest but he's coughing badly.

The lawyers sent your medical records from St. Mary's Hospital. You were really in bad shape after practice. I guess I can be thankful I was able to hold your hand and be by your side for 18 more days.

I just hope you weren't suffering. I hope you heard us tell you how much we love you and how special you are.

Keegan is having fun with her kitty. Tiger and the kitty are tolerating each other a bit now.

Grandpa Fincher called tonight. He is still very angry. I'd love to be able to say something to make him feel better, but I'm not able to find words for myself. If only I could glimpse what you are doing and how happy you are maybe I would feel better. But maybe not because I just miss you so. Good night, Kendrick . . . I love you—I love you—I love you—I love you—I love you!

October 21, 1995

Hi my Son—today I was very motivated. I think it was motivation to keep busy and not think about you being gone, but I did think of you a lot today just as I do every day.

I talked to Aunty Shelly. Her tests were good this week. She starts radiation in a week and a half and will be taking it for six weeks. I talked to Uncle Rolland (my brother), *too. We talked mostly about religion. I wish I knew what was beyond this life. There are so many questions. I want to be where you are so I can be with you for eternity or what we face after this life.*

Keegan got to go to Jenny's Halloween party this evening. She had a great time. I was thinking you would maybe have been going if you were here. They had a hay ride, played basketball and danced. It looked like a great time.

I called the prosecutor yesterday. I wanted to let him know that we really want felony charges. He doesn't think they will be able to do that. Even a misdemeanor will be difficult. I guess there was a boy *in Arizona that died three years ago from heat stroke. His parents were awarded a million dollar suit. The school has to pay $850,000 and the coaches pay $150,000.*

Dad's feeling better now. I pray there is a rapture and it is soon so I can be with you. I love you and miss you so. Good night, Kendrick . . . I love you.

October 24, 1995 – Tuesday

Today we went to Little Rock for Keegan's check up. It wasn't too bad. It seems I block out a lot, like a bad dream I want to forget. I saw the helicopter you were transported in to Little Rock. We didn't have to go in the hospital because Keegan's check up was in the building next door.

Keegan was being rather challenging at lunch today and I whispered to Dad that you were looking down saying, "See Mom, I always told you she was a brat." Yes, we have spoiled her. You always had to be the one to give in because you were older. Yes, we were really easy on her because of her surgeries and our worry. If you would have survived the heat stroke you would have been one spoiled child, too.

I've been reading a book on different religions and how they view life after death. It sure is confusing. How do I know what is the truth? Will I really get to be with you in eternity? Are you in heaven? This all makes me wonder—what is the meaning of life? What is the meaning of death?

I'm not sure if Dad and I are getting along. We don't talk much. You really brought him out of his shell and tough exterior and now you're not with us. Keegan and I are like pains in his side I think. I don't know how he can stand being home so much. There is so much about him that makes me angry and unloving lately and I have to search for any positives and sometimes I feel like I have to really stretch for a positive. But . . . this is hard. It is still hard to believe you are gone. How will our lives be in a year? Two years? Five years? Ten years? Now a part of our lives and dreams is gone. I feel like God has been cruel to us, but then we don't know the plan and we don't really know if this is actually a blessing. Maybe someday we will know. I pray that I can gather some good over your loss. What can that possibly be? My heart aches and my life is lonely and I am so sad.

As I cry I wish you were here so I could kiss you good night and tell you good night, Kendrick. I love you.

October 26, 1995

Dear Kendrick. I feel like asking Kendrick, Kendrick, my son, how I wonder where you are, like a diamond in the sky, up above the world so high. Where are you? How are you?

The investigator questioned Dad today. Doesn't sound like there will be charges filed. Doesn't seem right but I just said a prayer about it to have God intervene. I know I will accept whatever the decision is because no matter what happens to the coaches I don't get you back here with me on earth. Wouldn't it be neat that if a wrongful death was "righted" somehow the person would come back to earth? After being in heaven you probably would have no desire to come back, though.

I was remembering this evening how I always used to sing you the song "whatever will be will be . . . the future's not ours to see . . ." when you were little. I used to sing to you a lot when you were little. I haven't much to Keegan. Even last spring when you were doing your poem book you listed "You are my Sunshine" as your favorite song. When you were in the hospital I recorded it on one of the tapes I recorded for you. Could you hear the tapes? Did you hear my voice?

Tonight everybody from work went out to dinner. Nancy Hollenbeck's (friend from work) *son James sat across the table from us. He is nine and in 5th grade. Dad and I both thought he had hair like you. Colleen Cadreau had said how she always remembered what nice hair you had.*

I'm glad tomorrow's Friday. I've been staying up way too late every night.

I ran into Aileah and her mom at the mall on Sunday. She was wearing the cross earring that matched the one she gave you. She said they found the other one at the school. She said she would give it to us.

Aunty Shelly and I talked for a long time last night. We'd like to have the answers for everything. I wonder sometimes—when friends of the family in Minnesota stopped by Grandma and Grandpa's the day after your funeral I questioned why they could have four healthy sons . . . I went downstairs and cried after they left and told Dad it just wasn't fair.

Sometimes I think we watched you so closely you never learned that sometimes you have to look out for yourself. Unfortunately, your first day of practice was one of those days. Dad said that's why he never even had you mow the lawn much, because he didn't want you getting hurt. I get so angry sometimes but then it turns to sadness—there is so much I can't change—why? Why? Why?

Good night, Kendrick. I love you!!!

October 29, 1995

Today was my 36ᵗʰ birthday--the saddest birthday of my life. I wasn't feeling well either so we didn't go anywhere. We watched church on TV. Dad and Keegan baked me a birthday cake. When they gave me my cards I cried because you weren't here. You always liked birthdays even if they weren't yours. It was a sad, sad day. I spent a lot of time crying.

Grandpa Fincher called this evening. He's very angry. That doesn't do any good, though. We have to accept what happened, hard as that is, and move on with life. Aunty Robin called this evening, too. She said a 48-year-old man at her church had a heart attack and left behind eight kids. What sadness they have. There is so much sadness in the world.

Aunt Shelly starts radiation this week. So, I'm sure she had a sad day, too. She only sees her family on the weekends because she is getting treatments out of town.

There is so little in life that brings me joy and comfort lately. I always want to be with Daddy and Keegan. I like listening to Christian music and programs. I pray that God will find me worthy of heaven and that I can see you again. A program on TV this morning talked about the coming of Christ being soon. Life has little joy. I'm anxious for the glory of heaven.

We have Thanksgiving and Christmas coming up . . . my birthday was hard enough. There is a seminar at St. Mary's next Sunday on helping to cope through the holidays. I think Dad and I are going to go. Good night, Kendrick—I love you.

October 31, 1995

Halloween. I enjoyed getting the treats ready for the trick or treaters and having all the kids come to the door. Jenny took Keegan with her and her friends. She had a great time and got lots of candy. We missed you, though. Everything I do is with a tinge of sadness. There is always the thought that something is not right. It is your absence that has left emptiness.

When I hear the stories about life after death I feel a surge of joy in my heart that I will be with you again. It gives me a great sense of peace and anticipation to have the hope of seeing you again. For some reason tonight I'm feeling like I'll be seeing you soon. But, that may be me and my denial thoughts. Or is it forgetfulness, or confusion, or just wishful thinking? I'm picturing you with your green and black striped t-shirt and jean shorts. And now I'm crying because I can imagine you . . . but you're not here. But, maybe you're so close to me in spirit that I should feel your presence.

Today seemed like the most normal day I have had at work since before your accident. I was busy and started to feel like actually being involved. Still, I don't think more than 15 minutes go by without me thinking about you. I still have your photos in my office. I heard Dad telling someone he'd like to get your photo age progressed but I know just how you would look as you aged—just like your Dad minus the freckles and with blond hair, a really handsome man. Best of all, I know you would have always been as kind and sweet as ever. I'm sure you fit in perfectly in heaven, but I miss your kindness and sweetness here on earth. I'm sure I didn't tell you often enough what a great kid you were.

I remember our trip to California the last weekend in July just a week before your accident. You were lying in bed in the hotel room watching TV and you left a mess around you. You said to me, "I'm a real slob."

I said, "No, you're not a slob, you're just acting like one." Then you got up and cleaned up the whole room so when the maid came she only had to leave towels. I always told you that you could do anything you would set your mind to. You were content with a lot of the simple pleasures in life. I wonder what pleasures are part of your heavenly life?

Good night, Kendrick. I love you!!!! I miss you!!!!!

Chapter 5

I Am So Mad!

I don't care if it is God's will! I don't care if he is in a better place! I want him here with me! People think I am okay, but I am not.

There is a time frame after you lose a child where people will be there for you. They will bring you meals, clean your house, and do all sorts of things for you if you let them. Take advantage of it all you can because it will end! Then, you will be faced with endless days of wondering where everyone went and dealing with people that think you are really okay. You are not okay and their inability to understand what you are going through will just make you madder.

November 4, 1995

My heart is aching so much tonight. I have been angry all day. I am so sad you are gone, but also angry. I was sad but yet the tears wouldn't come because I was angry. For some reason I kept thinking about seeing your body after you were dead. They made us leave your room after you died while they removed the respirator and the other equipment. When we went back in about an hour later the room was all empty except for the bed and a chair. And there you were lying lifeless on the bed. You were so blue it hardly looked like you. Your hands were cold. Your body was all cold and blue. I lifted up the sheet to see your legs and they looked normal. And your hair, I could run my fingers through your hair and that was the same. I'd run my fingers back over your forehead and through your hair so much in the hospital because I remember when you were little you always wanted me to do that when you were falling asleep.

Keegan just handed me your Mariners shirt to comfort me. She's been trying to comfort me as I've been sobbing. I guess she figured I needed the shirt so she took it off and handed it to me. She's comforted by wearing your shirt to bed and sleeping on your pillow.

We got another notice about a Compassionate Friends meeting on Monday evening. I don't think I can go. Two families are noted on the notice—they lost their kids in 1969 and in 1983—are they still mourning? How long do I have to hurt? I don't like to cry so much so I avoid thinking too much about my sadness.

I'm reading a book on children's near death experiences. It really makes me wonder so many things. Did you have a choice to go to heaven or stay on earth? Did you have a near death experience before your final death? I know you were close to death for so long. I have so many questions for you but I know when I join you in heaven none of that will matter anyhow. Is your spirit really next to me whenever I think of you? Good night, Kendrick. I love you!!

November 7, 1995 – Tuesday

Today was a day filled with anger and sadness. People said it gets harder and I think I know what they mean now. Reality is sinking in. I'm also angry because we met with the prosecutor and it doesn't sound like they will have any charges. I can't believe that there wasn't any negligence.

Robin told me some people put antifreeze in dog's dishes on Halloween night and they are being charged with a felony. But I guess it is okay in Arkansas not to let a child drink water! How will we ever get this place fixed?!! Why did we have to find out so harshly about football and town politics?

I was watching church on TV this evening and the topic was on life's storms and the power of prayer. Prayer did not work for us. We didn't get to keep you here with us. Why? How come you had to go? I told myself all those niceties about you being chosen and now I'm thinking all that is a bunch of crap. People make up all that stuff to survive the death of a child or loved one. It got me through the first two months, but, now what? It's soon the holidays and I don't have you here.

I read a small book on attitudes tonight—just a book full of quotes, but I needed an attitude adjustment. I still need more, though. I don't feel good on the inside or the outside. I'm tired, I'm sad, I'm mad, I'm missing you, and I'm basically very unhappy. I'm so unhappy that I don't like to see others happy.

I almost called Rochelle and told her to quit being depressed and feeling sorry for her plight. I'd give anything to have cancer and have you back instead. It's funny how other's trials seem more trivial than ours. I remember after you died and I had to go to the store. There was a lady talking about her toe nail surgery and all the details and pains she had with that. The focus in life is sure strange. People work too hard. They get obsessed with things, they plan too far ahead and they act like they are going to live forever. Well, all we have is today. My days are sad and lonely without you. Poor Keegan will soon tire of comforting me because I have been crying so much lately.

As I read through my notes it sounded like Keegan was taking care of me. After all, she was only seven years old at the time and had lost her big brother. Comforting her mother would have been a huge charge for a young lady that needed comforting of her own. I asked Keegan recently and she said she doesn't remember anything about that time after Kendrick died. My guess is that we comforted each other just by being close to each other.

Well, my dear son, I need your spirit of comfort and love. Good night, Kendrick. Good night, my son. I love you.

November 10, 1995 – Friday

Well, your spirit did comfort me and get me through what I thought was going to be very tough. There will be no criminal charges filed in your death. The prosecutor could not find willful intent and there were no laws broken. He said there was wrongdoing, just not criminal wrongdoing. We need to work on changing the laws.

Channel 5 talked to us yesterday. The newsperson is the real nice man that filmed your funeral so I felt comfortable that he would be sensitive to our feelings, and he was. He did a nice story. He even said Channel 5 will help with a fundraiser if we want to do one for your ballpark.

We got snow tonight. Just three months ago it was so hot you collapsed and now snow. Talk about extremes.

Thanksgiving is only a week and a half away or almost two weeks I guess. I'm sure glad all of Dad's family is going to be here. Otherwise, I would really be dreading four days at home and a very lonely Thanksgiving. Keegan wants to bake chocolate chip cookies this weekend. I think I will bake some pies, too. Grandpa

Fincher's favorite is apple pie. Your favorite was lemon cream and you ate that whole lemon cream pie in California the weekend before your accident.

I sure wish you were here so we could really talk. You were always so enjoyable to talk with because you were so level-headed and rational. When I had a bad day you always helped me feel better by helping me realize it was really no big deal.

Well, I'm very sleepy . . . good night, Kendrick. I love you.

November 12, 1995 – Sunday

Yesterday we took your friend, Aileah, out to lunch and then she came with us to Hobby Lobby and the Fayetteville Mall. We enjoyed having her with us. I can see why you liked her. Some of her traits remind me of you.

I still can't believe it's real. I feel so cheated, but I shouldn't feel cheated. I should feel grateful. I guess I feel cheated because I know what I'm missing. I'm missing having you around with all the joy you brought to my life. So I should feel thankful that I had you for 13 years rather than cheated you are gone. You didn't come with any promises, did you? I still miss you and I cry often because I'm sad, and sometimes I'm mad and crabby and angry.

We made up a toddler bed for Keegan in our room. She and I made a blanket to match our comforter. I thought she should not sleep on the floor anymore. I know she won't be sleeping downstairs anytime soon.

After Kendrick died, Keegan started sleeping in our room on blankets next to our bed. The kids' bedrooms were downstairs and she didn't want to be that far from us, nor did we want her that far from us.

We tried a new church today—First Christian Church. It was okay. The people were very nice. It was communion Sunday.

I wonder what you know up there in heaven. Dad said he saw three shooting stars on his walk with you and Shadow tonight. Is it coincidence or is it a sign from you?

Kendrick's dad used to take a walk with the dog every evening as his special time to think about Kendrick. So, we called them his walks with Kendrick.

I haven't found many pennies lately. I like when I find them as I think you may be thinking of me.

Good night, Kendrick. I love you.

November 18, 1995

Hi Honey. I haven't written to you all week. It's hard to know what to say sometimes. I think about you a lot and think of things I'd like to say to you.

A boy on your football team came over yesterday. His mom called earlier in the week. He quit practice and football on the first day. He said he walked off the field and others followed. I wondered why you didn't quit, but I know you weren't a quitter at anything and you really wanted to play football. Just like in the hospital you were a fighter till the end.

I still replay events in my mind and wonder why things couldn't have ended up differently. I'm reading a book entitled <u>When Bad Things Happen to Good People</u>. The author doesn't believe God chooses for people to die. So that even confuses me more. I don't understand how he could allow your death. He could have *influenced you to quit, the coaches to let you have water and to have you shower, could have influenced Dad to take you to the emergency room rather than coming home and calling the hospital, could have caused you to collapse on the field so an ambulance would have been called sooner. He could have healed you in the hospital.*

Our house is still so lonely, but we are getting familiar with your absence. We got a card from a family that lost their eleven-year-old son due to an asthma attack at school the end of September. They must be so very sad and yet they took the time to write. I will call them soon. I just don't know what to say.

Yes, even though I just went through a loss of a child, it is so difficult to know what to say to grieving parents. My advice to those of you reading that have not lost a child: just listen or share special memories. After a child dies the last thing a parent wants to hear is that it is "God's will," or that "he/she is in a better place," or any of the other comments people make that they think might be comforting, but really don't offer much consolation. I remember the most comfort I received from a visitor was when they just listened or shared a special memory with me. The ones I remember with anger are those that thought they needed to give me advice on how to handle the loss—even from parents who had lost a child.

At Kendrick's funeral in Minnesota a lady stopped me and sort of blocked my way so I couldn't walk forward, took my hands, and talked to me for at least five minutes on how it would all be okay. She had lost a child earlier and thought she needed to take MY time at MY son's funeral to give HER advice to ME. I do not remember a thing she said to me, only that she took up time that I would have liked to be visiting with family. There are also well-meaning people that think just because I have lost a child that I should call someone else and give them advice. What I know is that they will call me if they want that information.

Each person grieves differently and each person has different needs to get through the grieving process. What I did enjoy were books that I could read when I was ready to read them. As I was listing the additional resources at the back of this book, I was reminded of the kind friends that gave me the books and wrote a note in the front of them

Next Thursday is Thanksgiving. I'm learning to say thanks for what we have. How blessed we were when you were here with us and we didn't realize how excellent our life really was. And now—I'm learning to be thankful for what we have. Memories. They just don't quite fill the void.

Good night, my special son—Kendrick—I love you.

November 21, 1995 – Tuesday

Yesterday was a sad day. All days are sad but yesterday was especially sad. I had to leave work and come home and cry. I feel like I don't like anything anymore except Keegan—my job, Dad, relatives, me—I feel pretty lost and confused. I had a good cry and I pouted all evening and I felt better today. I think I may make it through this week.

Thanksgiving will be hard. We will be missing you and we'll have a houseful of people here. But that will keep me busy and not think so many sad thoughts. Dad won't even bring up your Sega and Lego's for your cousins to play with, and we're not letting anyone in your room. I'm sure you wouldn't mind but we want it to stay the same.

Keegan has been talking about you a lot. She misses all the fun you used to have together—Lego's, GI Joes, forts—she even misses you babysitting her. I asked her how she keeps from crying and she said

she just plays with her kitty. She's putting on your Mariners shirt to sleep in now.

I wonder if you celebrate any holidays in heaven. Is your death day your birthday in heaven? Is it a reason to celebrate?

November 29, 1995

Oh, I just couldn't write anymore—haven't been able to write. Writing is admitting you are gone and I can't talk to you. How strange this is that you are gone. I talked with Grandma last night and she said it's getting harder for her. I did read that the fourth to seventh months are the hardest because that is when the reality sets in. I wrapped up your present for Grandma so it is ready to mail. Remember your cross-stitch teddy bear in the Christmas stocking you started for Grandma two years ago? Well, you never quite finished it but I had it framed for her just the way it was. I know she will love it but she will be sad, too.

We had a nice Thanksgiving with Daddy's family here. Derrick's family came over for Thanksgiving dinner, too. You would have had so much fun, but who knows what our holiday would have been if our lives hadn't been shattered this year. We may have been just us four again. That was always fine and a nice Thanksgiving. Your cousins rode the three-wheeler a lot.

We got copies of the prosecutor's files. I haven't been able to bring myself to read them. Grandpa Fincher did and I could tell it was upsetting. Dad read them, too, but he was aware of most of the information anyway. The lawyers say the school says that the paramedics didn't treat you properly when they arrived at the house. So they say the paramedics are to blame for your death. I just want to focus on prevention and let the lawyers worry about the blame. I just know you are gone and you shouldn't be.

I have lots of flashback memories of the 18-day nightmare. When I met you at the hospital you looked just like you were sleeping on the stretcher, not uncomfortable or in pain. Your blond hair so beautiful, your beautiful face. I remember I ran my hand through your hair and just told you I was there. I didn't know what to say. I was scared. It was a short ride up in the elevator and they sent me to the waiting room to spend an agonizing time until I could see you again. Then it only got worse, but, now you know all of that. I hope you weren't in pain. I wish you could have heard me and yet I wish you were out of it because of the terror you may have had in your heart.

I remember once when you were about nine—I think it was after your cousin Kevin died—I was talking with you and tucking you into bed and you were crying saying you didn't want to die. I remember thinking how special you were and hoped that you wouldn't be one of those that died young because one always hears about the good dying young.

I still question why we had to have this sorrow—why you? God only knows and maybe there is no purpose. Just fate, just unplanned destiny? You had so many dreams and goals.

Well, my darling, it's bedtime . . . I stay up so late now. I don't like to go to bed at night. We'd be telling you to get to bed so you can get up for school in the morning and asking if you finished your homework. Remember when we went to my office to use the computer one evening last spring? We stayed late and did your poem book. I'll always remember that as a special evening. We had a good time and I treasure that book. I have so many memories I treasure. I'd rather have you, though. But, my dear, you are in the Lord's hands.

Good night, my son. I love you.

Chapter 6

A New Calendar Year Without Kendrick

The pages on the calendar are milestones. Making it through Thanksgiving and Christmas were two huge milestones. Now, another milestone greeted us . . . a new year starting without Kendrick.

January 20, 1996

I've just been looking through your photo albums and crying. I haven't written to you for so long. I think a sense of denial just to get through the holidays. It's the new year now. I'm glad to say goodbye to the sorrow of 1995, but how do I get going on this new year without you? I was reading from the Bible a little earlier. What if heaven is not there? What if you're just gone? Where is heaven? It must be very far away in another solar system. I miss you so much. I miss your jokes, your laughter, your hugs, your kisses, your sweetness, the way you said, "Mom" and "Good night, Mom, I love you."

We've done a lot since the end of November. Are you watching over us? We've been trying to keep busy to keep the sorrow away. The frames we ordered for family and friends in your memory were beautiful. They will be nice memories.

After Kendrick died we had wooden frames made to hold his photo that were etched with "Remembering the spirit of compassion, kindness and friendship to all" along with his name and birth and death dates. We gave them to some family members and special friends.

We can't decide what to do about a ballpark or other memorial. We're considering just setting up a foundation for now. We're going to order sports drink bottles with instructions on how to avoid heat illness.

We meet with the lawyers on Monday to find out what they recommend.

It feels good to be writing to you again. I don't know if it is healthy for healing, but I imagine it is because it helps me talk through some of my feelings.

Aunty Shelly is doing okay right now. I hope she stays healthy. Her family needs her here.

Well, Dear, I guess I'm able to face my recovery from my grief again. So, I will continue to write in here more often again. Your birthday would have been in a week and a half. You'd be continually making your requests and pestering me about what I was buying you.

I love you, Sweetheart. I miss you so much and you know you are on my mind almost constantly. Sometimes I'm okay and sometimes I'm not. Sometimes I feel like I try to pretend it didn't happen, and sometimes I wonder if your life was a dream rather than losing you a nightmare.

Well, Hon, I'm going to start on my new year. I'm going to make my list of goals for the year for me and also what I want to do in your memory. So good night, Kendrick—I love you!

January 30, 1996 – Tuesday

Kendrick—I miss you so. I keep waking up early in the mornings and thinking about you. I can't believe I won't see you again. I won't see you grow up, go on dates, drive a car. At church on Sunday a young man that came to visit us after you died came and sat next to us and I was looking at his hands and how much I miss holding your hands. We placed flowers at the front of the church on Sunday---fourteen white roses in memory of your birthday. Dad is supposed to go get one so we can dry it and save in memory.

I got the sample of the water bottles we're considering distributing for all the sports programs with heat stroke prevention information. We're meeting with the lawyer on Thursday to talk about setting up a nonprofit foundation. The lawyer from last Monday cancelled our appointment and we're meeting with them on Saturday regarding a suit or whatever they recommend.

Your sister is doing great. She's growing up so fast. I remember you at that age changing from a little boy into a young man.

After church on Sunday a couple came up to us and asked us if we were the Fincher's. They were Marty and Bill Keeling. Their son, Andy, was there at practice with you and he had heat exhaustion. He passed out behind the school and a UPS driver found him. He was treated and released at the hospital. Wonder why he was saved and you weren't. What did we do wrong? Why would God spare him and not you? Is Andy lucky or were you lucky to go to heaven early? I don't like waiting for answers!! What I wouldn't give to replay time and have a different ending to last summer.

Daddy's on the phone talking with Uncle Kenny (Mike's uncle from Chicago). *We had fun seeing him at Christmas. We told him how much you thought of him.*

Life . . . I was listening to a tape by Wayne Dyer the other day and he said, "We think we are human beings with a spiritual side. What we forget is that we are really spiritual beings having a human experience." But, it's that fear of the unknown. Now I know you are there in the unknown. The unknown I like to believe is heaven and God and all things good. I believe that you are cared for and loved and peaceful in a blissful life. Faith . . . that which we don't see and yet believe. I have faith I will see you again. Good night, Kendrick. I love you!

February 5, 1996 – Monday

This weekend and today have been sad. You would have been 14 today. We had our candle memorial at home and we released a Happy Birthday balloon to you with a note from us. Did you watch? We cried lots. Keegan was even crying and she hasn't cried much. She said later that she wished she would have sent your valentine up with the balloon. She said she didn't want you to go away—she wanted you to stay down here with us.

I was wondering in church yesterday why Keelings got to keep Andy. It doesn't make sense. Why couldn't you survive too? I guess we'll know when we join you.

Aileah was over for lunch on Sunday. She finished the painting and it is very special. (She painted a portrait of the family for us.) *We gave her the frame we had made. All these activities seem so strange and still like a bad dream.*

I get so sad, mad, angry, depressed. Then, I'm okay sometimes. People always ask how I'm doing and I just say okay. I can't talk about it. How can you be okay after a child dies? I miss you so much. Kendrick . . . you were so special. I remember once you wrote on a card to me that you liked when I told you that you were special. Well, you were. We were so blessed.

I'm in Atlanta tonight. It was hard to leave again today—on your birthday and a reminder of last time I flew here and you had your accident. I met the lady this morning that tracked me down at the hotel. She gave me a hug and I thanked her.

Life is so strange. You were so important to us. People die every day that are important to someone. The world is full of so many people, all of us significant to only a few people and in those lives a tremendous void is left.

Happy Birthday, Honey. I guess your earthly birth date holds no significance for you anymore. For us it will always be a bittersweet day, kind of like every day we have to face without you, but one in which we feel your absence even more. I love you, Kendrick. I miss you. I can't wait to see you again.

Good night, Kendrick—I love you.

February 13, 1995

Hi Honey. This is sure tough. I'm a real mess. I'm feeling like I've lost total control of everything. I'm trying so hard to maintain my focus at work and it's a real struggle. I forget easily, I'm feeling no confidence. My boss gave me a poor evaluation and mentioned a potential reassignment. Kendrick . . . I'm about over the edge. My strength is totally sapped. I called and scheduled an appointment with the psychologist again. We can't move and I know there are few jobs around here that pay well. So, what do I do? How can I just get over this? Why do people think I'm over this??????!!!!!!

The books are all right. They said it gets harder four to seven months after a death. I couldn't see how that could possibly be true, but it is true.

Rose just called. She scolded me for not having an answering machine. She may come visit or she wants to go somewhere with me. It's hard for me to be away from Dad and Sis, though.

I just want to become a hermit. I want to crawl in bed and cry. I don't want to take care of myself even.

Baby—life has sure gotten painful. I'm too sad and depressed to even self-talk my way out of this. Well, I'm sure there are people who would love to trade their problems for mine. Why is it when we are down it is so easy to continue to think about all our woes? Let's see, I have a lot to be thankful for: Dad, Keegan, I had you, your Grandma and Grandpa, Aunty Shelly is doing okay. I have a close family, a great job (even though it's stressful and I feel it may be slipping away), we have a great house in a great neighborhood. Oh, I guess there's a lot more, too. Why am I so depressed? You!!!! I miss you so much. It just is not right. You should not be gone. I don't understand why!!! I wonder how I can live this life so lonely. Good night, Kendrick. I love you. I miss you.

April 1, 1996

I feel like I have been in an underground tunnel the past months. What about you? I wonder about you often—where you are and what you are doing. Happiness is hard to come by anymore. It seems like life has been hard from so many directions. I wonder if that's because I've been so depressed and stuck on being miserable. I've started to tell myself, "Today was a great day and tomorrow will be even better." It's a lie but I felt like maybe my life should be turning around for the better. It was funny---a simple thing like Keegan getting an award at school last week for bringing up her grades—she was so proud to get the award (a t-shirt) and we were so proud to watch. So I keep repeating: "Today is a great day and tomorrow will be even better"—and variations of that to keep me looking for the good.

The news came that Rochelle has the cancer in her liver and bones now. As shocking as that was it made me stop my wallowing in my own misery and refocus a little. She's thankful for each day she can have with her family and I'm being so miserable over life and its sorrows that I'm not even reaching out to attempt to enjoy life. I know work is contributing to my depression also. It is just too much on top of dealing with missing you.

The lawyers talked to one of the doctors from Little Rock last week. She said the coaches and school did a lot wrong. So they're going to sue. I did a draft of the brochure and sports bottle, too, so Dr. Schaefer is reviewing that now. Dr. Schaefer is the doctor that treated you when you arrived at St. Mary's. Then we'll get those printed and distributed in your memory.

Grandma is having a hard time and Aunty Robin, also. Losing you and Rochelle's cancer have really been taking a toll on the family. I pray that Rochelle will get a miracle. We prayed so hard for one for you—still can't figure out why we couldn't keep you. I guess God had a higher purpose through your death.

We had Cauthens over for dinner a couple of weeks ago. It was fun to see them and visit. We gave Derrick the frame in your memory. Sue called and said they really liked it and they put it in the living room. We dropped off Mr. Zach's (Kendrick's favorite teacher from Harvest Park Middle School in California) *when we were in California and we mailed Jonathon's* (Kendrick's friend from

Colorado). *We haven't heard from them yet. Mr. Zach wasn't there when we stopped. It was hard to visit California. Made me wonder why we ever left. Would you still have been with us if we hadn't moved? I heard on the radio this morning that "God knows the number of our days." So, I guess this was the plan??*

Grandpa Mac (Mike's grandfather in Chicago) *said he saw you—he said, "I saw the boy," and asked how his parents were doing. He almost died in January—did he visit you in heaven? I can't wait to talk to him in May when we go to Chicago.*

Well, Sweetie, keep on watching over us and have God bless us. We need some peace and happiness and health for Rochelle, too. You know, I thought if she dies, she gets to see you. I told Dad it should be me because at least I'd be with you. He reminded me that he and Keegan still need me. Rochelle must be having a hard time. They only gave her six months to live. She's going to try more chemo and her cleansing diet. What pain and suffering she has to endure. I just don't understand how God allows this. Maybe you can watch over her, too. You probably already are.

I miss you . . . I don't cry as much, but I avoid situations that will bring the tears. Good night, Kendrick. I love you.

April Fool's Day—I wish this pain and your leaving was all a joke!!

April 11, 1996

Well, today was the big day the civil suit made the news. I feel sorry for the coach you liked. But I guess he wasn't feeling too sorry for you when you were thirsty. I'm sure he feels real sorry now—I hope he will be okay. I do forgive the coaches because I have a feeling of empathy for them to have to live with what they did. They had to have known they could harm you. It all still seems like a dream. I was watching the news Dad taped and it seems just like that—like I'm watching a story on TV. It seems like a dream that you were ever here because I can't believe you are gone.

Grandma and Grandpa Roseland are really down. Life has been hard for all of us, but I can't listen to them complain. I know they seem helpless and I know everything seems hopeless with Rochelle and they are frantically trying to save her just like we did for you. But, is it meant to be? Why does God allow this to happen? I don't know how we can all lose another family member. I feel very numb, yet I'm functioning well day-to-day, not productively, though. I think I use all my energy keeping up my spirits.

I guess there is a dance at school tomorrow. I wonder if you would be going. I'm sure all the girls would want to dance with you. You were so kind and handsome.

I imagine life can be good again. At least I can imagine that now and not only wonder how I can even live. I guess that means I'm getting better. Sometimes when I'm feeling like I'm seeing the light and I'm out of the dark cloud of sadness, the reality smacks me in the face. I'm sleepy, so good night, Kendrick. I love you. Where is my good night kiss??

April 19, 1996 - Friday

Well, Son, it's been a busy week. I guess business can help push me forward in life--or pull me forward. I lit a candle at St. Patrick's Cathedral for you on Monday in New York City. Rose gave me a prayer card she got in the gift shop there that made me cry.

I had to attend a training session in New York City and my friend Rose Peterson from Minnesota met me there to spend a couple extra days. I really was in no mood to travel. I had to endure a managers' meeting at Disneyworld in December after Kendrick died. The only good thing about that trip was that my friend Sandy Miller from Chicago was also there.

On this particular trip I was seated next to an elderly lady on the flight from Arkansas to Dallas. We started talking about children and the topic of Kendrick's death came up. She said she had lost both a husband and a child and the loss of a child is far greater than the loss of a spouse. This made the trip worth it . . . to get those comforting words. Although they don't seem like comforting words, it helped me realize that the pain was real and I was not alone.

I keep thinking about how I can't see you again. The topic of children came up at dinner last evening at my training session. So I talk about my children . . . I have two, but my son died last year. At first, it never fails, people are shocked. But I can't deny I have two kids. Sure I could say one and avoid the questions, but I like to talk about you. You were, and even still are, a big part of my life.

I'm on the plane headed home from New York City. It has been six days since I was home. I guess it was good to be away from work but I miss Dad and Keegan. I think I am going through an anger stage because I have been so very angry lately. I'm mad at the world because you are gone. I was so cranky with Rose on Tuesday. I'm feeling sorry for myself. I wonder why I had to lose you. And then, with everything else going on with work and Rochelle, it is just more than I want to have to deal with. I wonder what the purpose of all this is. How strong is God trying to make me?

Keegan missed me this week. She says she has trouble going to sleep without me to cuddle with her. So she's sleeping with the mice stuffed animals. (These were some stuffed animals that Mike had given me when we were dating. I don't really remember why she considered them comforting. However, recently I asked her if she wanted them and she took them home with her. They are over thirty years old now!) *I'm bringing her a stuffed rabbit from Boston and a Statue of Liberty book. It seems strange not to buy for you. I still forget sometimes and think, "Oh, Kendrick would like that--I'll have to buy it." Sometimes I even think of buying something I see and just pretending for awhile that you're waiting at home for me.*

I'm trying to figure out this grief stuff . . . I know so many people get through it because so many parents lose a child. But how? I guess the days continue to grow into months, the months into years, and the pain becomes less. But now, I still think of kissing your soft cheek with the peach fuzz on it. Usually a quick peck, but I always gave you a goodbye kiss.

We heard one of the coaches was reassigned to only teaching duties. Not much news on the case. We've had some positive feedback that we're doing the right things. We meet with the senator and state representatives next Wednesday so we can talk about what to do.

May 16, 1996 – Thursday

Mother's Day was a sad day. We had planned to be gone for the weekend so I would have a diversion. But Olivia and Jim called and were able to come so we stayed home because we wanted to have them over. They left Sunday morning. I was too sad to go to church. I knew I wouldn't be able to handle all the mother talk.

Andrew Cozart—a tax attorney—is going to set up your foundation for cost. There are some great people in this world. The other attorney we spoke with said it would be a minimum $5,000!!!! Wow!!

Your pamphlets are ready too. And the sports drink bottles will be here on the 30ᵗʰ. That'll be nice to have them before we leave for Minnesota. It helps to keep busy doing activities in your memory. Then, the absence doesn't hurt so much. Well, what do I mean—it still hurts! It's painful. I'm very angry now. The troubles at work were sort of the last straw for me. But, I think I'm on the rebound a little now. Just so Rochelle gets well. I don't want to face any more sorrow. It makes me feel numb.

Dad is going on a field trip with Keegan tomorrow to Lake Atalanta. They are both pretty excited. I remember the field trips I went on with you. Those are some great memories. Spring is so nice. It's nice to see nature coming to life.

Kendrick, remember when you were little and I sang to you when you were going to sleep? Your favorite song was "You are my Sunshine." I also sang "Whatever Will Be Will Be" except I changed "when I was just a little girl" to "boy"—it's a good thing we don't know what will be. It's good we can get over the past sorrows and not know our future sorrows because life would be too unbearable otherwise. Live in the present—live in the moment!! Yeah—me, I worry a lot—what will happen if? What would have happened if? It doesn't really make sense to worry, does it, because whatever will be, will be!!!!

A hug and a kiss would be nice. Thank God for the memories. Good night, Kendrick. I love you. Tomorrow we leave for Chicago for the weekend.

June 12, 1996 – Wednesday

"Ya, I really like this place"—I dreamt that was on a piece of paper in your handwriting. I liked that—I wondered if you could send

me a message in my dreams. I had never had a dream about you until about two weeks ago. I dreamt I was at work and everyone was going out after work so I was considering going out. I called home and you and Keegan were supposed to be home and there wasn't any answer so I thought I better go home. I went home and the only person there was a grey-haired older lady that I didn't know and the phone rang and it was you. You were crying. I said, "Honey, what's wrong?" You were just sobbing hysterically and then I woke up. So that dream alarmed me. Don't know what that could mean though.

So much has been happening in the last month. The water bottles and pamphlets are all being distributed through the park district. People are hearing about the foundation and that is getting attention. There have been articles in the newspapers and on the television news and someone nominated us for "people of the week" so that will be on the television news tomorrow. I know we're doing what you would want.

I hope you can help watch out for your sister. I want her safe and healthy and I always worry about her because of her shunt. You remember because we always spoiled her so much and worried about being careful. Now you, our healthy, strapping son is gone. Life is full of irony! Please help watch out for her. I worry about that dream with you crying—were you trying to say something? Keegan? Daddy? Rochelle? I can't bear any more sorrow. Life has given me what I have so far. I have been blessed in many ways, too, but it's easy to overlook the blessings when something sad happens.

I'm thankful I had you. I was blessed to know you and have you a part of my life. We're just to live each day like it is our last and treat each person we meet or deal with like they could die today or tomorrow. What a kinder world this would be, huh?

I was in Chicago this weekend and I could not resist going into the store where I picked out that leather jacket you wanted. I looked for the style you wanted and I found it. Once again I had the impulse to buy it and just pretend I could bring it home to you. We went to Minnesota at the end of May. Your memorial stone and bench are in place. It looks very nice—but, wow—to see your son's memorial stone! Your urn was ready, too. So now that sits on Dad's dresser.

Jenny Brandon (niece from Minnesota) *is staying with us this month. It's so nice to have her here. It helps to liven up the house a little. She fills your spot at the table. Well, no, she sits in your spot—your spot can never be "filled" by anyone.*

I am continually amazed at the depth of loss I feel. I can't even explain or find words to express. Right now I picture it like a climber at the bottom of a dark cavern pulling their way up a rope.

I guess the lawsuit will proceed. The judge made them take out one part, though, that was important for the case—the lawyers said it will be more difficult now.

Well, life continues to pull, or yank, me forward. It's pulling me too fast sometimes. I think when I'm depressed I need to keep a slower pace. Can't pile too much on myself or I get overwhelmed easily.

Well, Son, time to go sleepy. Will I see you in my dreams tonight? What an unbelievable life this is—spiritual beings having a human experience.

I miss you . . . Good night Kendrick . . . I love you. I love you. I love you. Good night, Kendrick – I love you!

July 12, 1996

Some days I think I should still wake up from this dream. We have been so busy I haven't had time to reflect . . . but sometimes that is for the best. I can go for awhile now without feeling so helpless. I don't feel as guilty anymore if I forget about you for a few hours and focus on work or something else. We still haven't touched your room. I don't go in there very much because it is too painful. Then I know you were really here and now you are really gone. If I don't go in there, sometimes it feels like you never were really here so you can't be gone. Somewhere my imagination is playing tricks. Dad spent the weekend with Uncle Ken at the lake in Minnesota. That's what you two were going to do sometime together. Uncle Randy was there with both his boys--doesn't seem fair you couldn't be there too. The mosquitoes were bad--where you are you don't get any of that.

I brought fireworks up to Grandma's house and Dad brought to the lake. I was thinking about you because you enjoyed them so much. Dad let them off on Thursday and I let them off on Friday--maybe you watched both shows.

Caleb (nephew from Minnesota) *was talking about you at Grandma's house--made me sad. He said you shouldn't have listened to the coaches. Easy to say, huh? Here we teach you to listen to those in authority and then you die because you did!! I hate to feel sorry for myself that you are gone because I'm sure you are very happy now, but I miss you. I wonder what you would look like today--how much would you have grown this past year? Would you have a girlfriend? I would hope not, but I'm sure they would be calling all the time. Would you still have the slow gait and the slumped shoulders? Would you still be combing your hair the same way and using gobs of my hairspray?! Would you finally be brushing your teeth daily so they didn't get crud on them? Would you be taking showers without us reminding you? Would you still* be enjoying Nintendo and Sega and watching TV? Would you still read your science fiction books? Would you have read more Og Mandino, the author you were just starting to enjoy? Would you still be building tents with your sister? She really misses that. Would you still be building elaborate Lego's and helping your sister build them? She misses that too. Would we have finished decorating your room the way you wanted it? We never did decide how to decorate your room here so it is not even decorated to your personality.

Remember the night before your accident and we went to Ryan's? You said there that you were going to quit eating red meat and just eat chicken and fish. You always enjoyed eating so much and it was fun when you enjoyed what I made. Dad said he missed having you say how good he cooked. He enjoyed your positive comments more than Keegan's or mine. Now ice cream will last weeks in the freezer instead of hours!!

I'm so anxious to be done with work and have some time to recover. I need to contemplate, reflect, relax, and rejuvenate from the inside out. I need to bring joy back into my life.

Rochelle is attempting to get in a cancer treatment program in Tulsa. She and Randy and the kids will be here next Tuesday. If she gets in the program, she and the kids will be staying with us for five weeks or more. I hope she gets in because there isn't much that is offering her any hope. I would also like to have her with me for awhile. I hope I can provide a relaxing, rehabilitating environment, with good food that she can eat and help nourish her body without damaging it.

I pray that God is blessing your heavenly home richly. We are still working on your foundation so you can bless people here on earth. You were such a blessing to us. Life doesn't seem fair, but then we have been more fortunate than many in other areas of our life *and I never questioned why life isn't fair when I'm getting what I want!!*

It's been rainy lately and I almost feel better when it's gloomy outside. That's the way it is supposed to be. How can the sun shine when my heart is broken? So, the rain just kind of fits my mood and it appears the world is agreeing with my feelings of sorrow.

Good night, Kendrick . . . How I love you.

July 15, 1996 - Monday

I'm feeling very blue today. I did last night, too. I believe Rochelle is just overwhelming me now. I feel this great sense of responsibility to be up for her and ensure she gets well. What will happen if she doesn't? How can I bear another loss? How can my family endure? Oh, I know we will--we're not supposed to get more than we can handle, right? It's just sometimes I can't even handle getting up and going to work. I really wanted to stay home today. I didn't sleep much. Grandpa Fincher and Cindy came yesterday to pick up Coquet--she said she was homesick, but I think Grandpa missed her. They left this morning already because Cindy had to be at a meeting at work tomorrow.

Coquet had come home with us after our trip to Minnesota and stayed for a few days. She had never been away from her parents for long so she got homesick quickly.

We went to Silver Dollar City on Saturday. We all had a nice time there. I know you would have loved the place, too. The evening show was great.

I hate going in to work--I know I should just quit because this is so unhealthy for me and so stressful to hate it. I keep thinking I should just get over it. Life isn't fair is it? Why do I feel sorry for myself? I really have had it pretty good. I don't think I used to take struggles so hard. But then, I never lost a child. I feel like after losing a child I have made enough earthly sacrifices and I should have a charmed life from here on out. I guess that life doesn't work that way. But how do I turn this around? Dad is so positive. I'm so fortunate to have him in my life or I know I would just fall to pieces.

Rochelle and the kids will be here late tomorrow. On Wednesday she will know if she will go through the treatment program in Tulsa. Sometimes I feel like she will not make it. Dad said he feels very confident she will make it. I don't think Rochelle believes she will survive and that is very detrimental. I'm trying to determine what I can do to make the time she spends with us a healing time. What do I cook, what do I buy, what do we do for fun, what do I do with the kids, what do I say, how do I react? I guess I'm worrying too much. Dad said I should just play it by ear and not do so much planning ahead. "Just go with the flow," he said. That's right . . . we'll see where the flow takes us and I will just deal with what gets in the way one step at a time. If it is sad, I can cry; if it is great, I can rejoice; if it is funny, I can laugh (can I still laugh?--this morning I don't feel like it); if it is angering, I can get mad; okay--I'll try to go with the flow and hope the flow is smooth and steady and positive and healing and that she stays with us on earth. I am scared to ask God to heal her, because what if the only way to heal her is to take her to heaven? I don't want her to go yet. I kept asking for your healing and then you died. I would have taken you with any handicaps. But God healed you and took you to heaven.

I guess Dustin (nephew from Minnesota) *would like to come and stay with us. I think I would like him to. Keegan likes him and she misses you so much. She said Dustin is fun like you were. If we aren't able to have any more kids, I want some other kids to come be my surrogate kids. I would take Rochelle's kids but it is best if they stay with Randy. Rochelle is worried Randy won't be able to take care of them. But we are far away from the rest of the family. However, I would love to have three more kids even if they are a bit of rascals.*

Keegan will be lonely today. This will be the first day she has been home alone with Dad since the end of May. First we had Jenny here and then Coquet. But she will only have two days of peace and then, hopefully, Rochelle and the kids will be here for the rest of the summer.

Rochelle sounded so sad last evening. She said she will be gone for eight weeks and she doesn't know what condition she will be going home in. A friend told her that maybe it is God's will if she doesn't live and that made her sad. That was a crazy thing for her friend to say.

Well, I'm starting to feel better talking to you. When you were alive I remember how I could have a bad day and you would help me feel better because you always took everything in stride. You went with the flow and didn't let everything upset you. I love you and I miss you. Your spirit lives on.

July 19, 1996 - Friday

Today is a big day. Rochelle is on her way to Tulsa to see if she can get in the study program. I know if she does, she will have some hope. If she doesn't, tonight will be a very sad evening. I am overwhelmed by a feeling of helplessness. I want to help her. To make it all better. To just think positively and positive things will happen. But how can I think positively? How can Rochelle think positively when she keeps getting worse? How can we help but have "worst case" thoughts when we have been so saddened by tragedy the past year. How can we turn the tide and begin to experience positive. How can the positive thoughts begin? One thought at a time--but I don't have the strength to think positively, the energy to put into getting well and thinking positive thoughts. Keegan wanted to buy a cute little black and white dress with a black jacket over it. When we bought it I thought it was darling and then I had a thought that maybe she would be wearing that to Rochelle's funeral. Where do these thoughts come from? I know Rochelle does not have much time left if she doesn't get in this study and it doesn't work. There I go again . . . I am thinking negatively. How can I convince myself she can make it? Does it even make any sense to think positively when she has cancer throughout her body? Where can that miracle come from? We didn't get a miracle with you--or did we? What is a miracle all about? I asked for your healing. But I also asked for you to be here on earth with us. I asked God to let us keep you here with us.

I could call Rochelle on the car phone, but I am scared to ask. If she isn't in the study . . . then what do I say? I can't make it all better. I have nothing to say. I guess, I say I'm sorry. But then I will cry and I can't cry because I have to make it through the day at work. I have to be strong. Or can I fall to pieces like I would really like to do? Can I lie in bed, cry, eat when I'm hungry, sleep when I'm tired, talk when I want to, sit in silence when I want to, yell when I want to, just do whatever I want, feel sorry for myself, feel sorry for Rochelle, feel sorry for her kids, for Grandma & Grandpa, for Robin and Rolland, for Randy? I guess there are others who are going through something worse so I shouldn't feel so sorry for myself--but I don't care--I want to feel sorry for myself. I want to pout, I want to cry, I want to shout, I want to hide from everyone for awhile. I just want to contemplate, read, and let my emotions do whatever they want whenever they want.

I can't concentrate at work. My mind is focused only on sustenance type activities. No planning, no competing, no improvements, nothing . . . just what I have to do to live. That is hard work in itself.

Rochelle has lost a lot of weight. Her hair is growing back a little bit. Raina and Roshan (Rochelle's two daughters) *were massaging her scalp last evening. I feel sorry for the kids. They need their mama. She needs to see them grow up.*

I'm feeling better after lamenting a bit. I guess I just have to get stuff off my chest from time to time and since you're not in an earthly body I don't have to upset you by pouring out my heart. Dad would think I was loony. He would tell me to read more positive books, to quit thinking negatively. He keeps so strong, but he won't talk about the sad parts of life very often. Does he avoid them? I think he has to face them sometime if he's just filing them in an unmarked file in his brain.

Well, Dear, today is Friday. I always appreciate Fridays because I have two family days after today. We don't have many plans for the weekend because we don't know if Rochelle can stay yet. If she stays, we will get situated for her living with us for eight weeks. If not, it will be sad and she will head home tomorrow. Don Camarda (Mike's friend) *from California will be here tomorrow night and stay through next Wednesday. Dad will enjoy having him here and hopefully it will be beneficial.*

Well, Dear, I will go . . . you're always in my mind and in my heart. The foundation is in the works and hopefully all will go well in establishing that and getting the funds available. You are such a special person. I love you. I miss you. Memories don't hold enough vividness to satisfy. Maybe I will see you in my dreams. I love you.

July 22, 1996

It has been almost 11 months you have been gone. I had another hysterical sobbing session last night. I really haven't had too many of those. Mostly quiet crying for short periods. I guess I needed a good cry. Sometimes I don't know what I am the most upset at and I start thinking about all I am sad about and it is overwhelming. Wish I could just "snap" out of it!! It is so hard to believe I had you and you are gone. I guess that's why the pain gets easier--because the memory fades. And that makes me sad because I don't want your memory to fade. This is just so unbelievable.

Rochelle got in the treatment program. When she got home on Friday she couldn't even walk. Randy had to carry her in the house and she slept upstairs on Friday. He even had to help her to the bathroom. We didn't tell Grandma because she would be way too worried. I was so sad. I felt so bad and I felt like she was dying and I got a glimpse of how sad it will be and how hard it will be if she deteriorates anymore. She said her pain was like labor. She took pain pills and it helped some. I even fed her because she was hungry and she couldn't get up to eat. She said it was embarrassing, but I don't mind. I will do anything for her. The pain got better over the weekend but she was still taking pain pills. Randy left on Saturday and that was very sad for her and the kids. Our friend Don is in town too and since he is a doctor that has been helpful for appeasing our fears over Rochelle's pain.

I don't know how Grandma has kept her strength up the last year living with Rochelle and helping her. The kids are good but they are a handful. Rochelle wants to help and she shouldn't. The kids want to sleep with her and sit on her lap and that hurts her. This must be very traumatic for them. Keegan has been very whiny lately. I don't know if it is because of the other kids around or because her shunt may be bothering her. It started when we got back from Minnesota after the Fourth of July and since then Coquet or Rochelle's kids have been here. I know Keegan likes lots of attention and she doesn't get as much attention or sleep when everyone is here.

Have a great day in heaven! I love you.

July 24, 1996

Last night before Keegan was going to sleep she said she was thinking of her thoughtful place and asked me if I wanted to know where that was. I said, "Yes."

She said, "It is heaven."

Roshan is scared for her mommy. She has been acting sick the last couple of days but I talked with her a few minutes last night before she fell asleep and was able to find out that she was scared. I thought it was kind of funny she has been lying around like she doesn't feel well, but yet no fever or other symptoms. I guess she just doesn't know what to do. We are all scared and don't know what to do. Just hope and hope and hope. Rochelle looked better yesterday. She seems to have her energy back. She didn't take a nap yesterday. Instead, she went shopping while Jenny babysat.

I've got a cold now, which I am sure is a result of all the stress. They are setting the date to review the investigation for August 16th, I believe. I made a list of what options they could take for settling and what my response should be. That way, if I am nervous or shocked, I can review my notes and know what to say. I've been trying to get in touch with the lawyer to check on distributing the water bottles and pamphlets to the football players on the first day of practice. I think it has been a cooler summer this year. We don't spend much time outside though.

Well, tomorrow is eleven months. The past year has been a blur that seems like a nightmare that I should be waking up from. I've got to remember that we're really spiritual bodies having an earthly experience. You are really home and I am just visiting this earth's plane. So, I shouldn't take anything too seriously except the growth of my spiritual existence. I've been really stretched this past year. Haven't broken yet, but I've been tried by some intense heat and pressure.

Well Sweetie, talk to you later. I love you.

August 6, 1996

I feel like I am crumbling like a house of cards that is shaking and ready to fall. What incident will be the final blow? Or will I get some positive supports to keep me going?

Dad and I had a good trip to California this weekend. It was sad in a way, though, because last year you were with us. We stayed in the same hotel. I was glad we had a different room layout so the memory wasn't too harsh. It was still rather melancholy. It was good to be away. We got to use first-class upgrades on the way home. That was really exciting. Dad hadn't flown in first class before. I only had a couple times before.

But then, back to work today. Why does it give me a pit in my stomach to have to go to work? I have no motivation. No direction, no inspiration to work. I used to be such a hard worker and so efficient. Now, nothing. I feel like I am just existing and wasting time and making a fool of myself.

This is one spot where I deleted some of my journal writings. I was having a really hard time at work through this time and I do not believe they were fair to me. However, it was not the company, it was individuals within the company and I was too deep in my grief to handle it well.

Grandma and Grandpa and Randy were in a car accident about 30 minutes away from home on their way here. Grandma was taken by ambulance to the hospital and x-rayed. They didn't see anything initially, but the State Patrol tracked her down yesterday and said she had to go back to the doctor as they noticed a mass on her x-ray. They didn't think it was a blood clot as it looks like it has been there awhile. I hope everything is okay. I don't have any energy to get upset or worry about anything else.

Rochelle seems better. She was pretty excited that one of her test results was better last week. It will be interesting to see if it is better this week. She is not limping as much and she looks so much better. Maybe our prayers are being answered!! I'd like to go with her to Tulsa this Friday, but my vacation days are so limited I think I need to save them. Maybe Dad can take her and the kids and then go to the park with the kids while she is getting treatment. I only have two vacation days left and we are planning to go to Denver in October.

Our house is in quite the disarray. Poor Dad is here all day with all the noise, but he is doing pretty well. We are going to meet for lunch today. Grandma, Grandpa, and Randy leave tomorrow afternoon.

Well, I feel better talking to you. I have been rehashing in my mind the hospital stay, the accident, etc., because yesterday was your first day of football practice last year. It was August 7th. Yesterday was August 5th, but it was that Monday. How I wish things had been different. I console myself that it must have been God's time for you rather than something we should have or could have prevented. But Why????? Life is just too harsh!! Living is too hard. I feel numb, slower, forgetful, can't concentrate--losing you is like losing a part of me--the alive part. What's left is this shell of a person trying to be an image of the person I was. I'm not the same. I feel like my friends are tired of me being sad and mad. Nobody wants to hear the same sadness over again. I know when people ask me how I'm doing, they want to hear "okay." So I say "okay". But I'm a long way from okay, a long, long way from okay. I do feel better away from work, so I know that is one stress I need to rid from my life eventually. I have to think longer term than right now. I have to focus, focus, focus, concentrate, concentrate, concentrate. I have to do what I have to do even as hard as it is. I just want to be home and sleep. Read. Cry. Laugh. Be at peace. Heal my heart. Find something that gives me happiness again. Keegan does, Dad does . . . so I need to be with them always. Maybe that is why I hate being at work so. Maybe it isn't work, just being away from family?

Well, Babes, I guess you aren't missing out on much in this troubled old world, but I sure am missing you.

I love you. I miss you.

August 7, 1996

One year to the date. Last night it hit me. I had to look at your pictures. I had to see you. I didn't care how much it made me cry. I just wanted to look at you and think about you. Dad came in and asked why I was punishing myself. Well, I don't know why I had to look at your photos that I knew would make me cry. I just wanted to see your face that fades from my memory. I wanted to think about how special you were.

I cried--sobbed--until I couldn't cry any more. Today I am very tired and very sad. I guess I didn't realize how much the "one year" date would bother me. Then I remembered that we went to Ryan's for dinner last night since we had 10 people and thought it would be easier. Well, we went to Ryan's last year on August 6th. During the night I thought about how you had woken up last year and weren't feeling good, and how the coach had called at 7:30 and you looked like maybe you were a little hesitant about going to football practice--how I wish I would have asked you, "Kendrick, what is the matter? Don't you want to be in football--did you change your mind?"

I remember not feeling good about you going to practice and I told Dad when I left early that morning that I was worried. I felt funny leaving that day. I remember thinking--"Am I sick, or just don't want to leave home today?" I wonder if it would have made a difference if I hadn't left that day. Would I have made you stay home? Would I have sent something with you to drink other than water? Would I have told Dad to go to the field to check on you? I think I would have been in a meeting at the office and Dad wouldn't have been able to reach me on my phone and he probably wouldn't have pursued having someone find me.

I keep thinking my being out of town was the way it was supposed to be so that I could meet you when you got to Little Rock. I don't think you knew I was there--or could you sense my presence even though you were drugged so? Could you feel my hand on yours or my hand on your head? You looked so helpless. The crew was so rushed and so short. They sent me to the waiting room. It was like a dream. Could this really be happening to my boy? This only happens in movies or to people I don't know. How can this be my son? How can Kendrick be lying there and not moving? What happened? God Bless Kendrick and make him well--I couldn't even pray, I was numb. Just--God Bless Kendrick and make him well. And now, could God only make you well if he took you to heaven?

Memories can be so pleasant and so harsh. I have pleasant memories of you, but they are so overwhelmed by the memories of your dying.

Good night, my sweet boy. It seems rather strange, last night, one year ago, you told me, "Good night, Mom. I love you." All I have now are the memories. I can't hear you. I'm not even sure I can feel your presence. I'm not sure what I feel. Just sad. Just very sad. Numb. Like I want to sleep and wake up and have my sweet son greet me and know that I just had had a terrible nightmare.

Good night, Kendrick. I love you. I miss you.

August 13, 1996

Oh--I was a nervous wreck today. I didn't sleep well last night. Yesterday morning I was feeling almost "normal" like I used to before you were gone, and then I had the realization that I will never be "normal" again. I am a changed person. I am more serious. I don't laugh much anymore. I don't smile much anymore. People used to say I was always smiling. That isn't the case much anymore. I don't know what is going to happen at work, but is my being this unhappy worth any price? Should I expect to be "happy?" Am I not doing enough to change my attitude? Life!! Dad has such a great attitude. I was such a crab last night to Rochelle's kids. Sometimes they make me angry, but I guess it isn't their fault they don't have structure and discipline. It's not Rochelle's fault either and yet I don't feel comfortable giving her suggestions because then she thinks that I think she is a bad mom. Dilemmas!!

Good night, Kendrick. Bless you, Son. I love you and I miss you!!

Chapter 7

One Year Later

I can't believe he is really gone. I made it through the first Thanksgiving, the first Christmas, the first birthday without him, the first Easter, the reminders of what we were doing last year at this time, and "the day." The clock clicks 10 a.m. It has been one year. One year ago I was standing by his hospital bed saying goodbye. Not goodbye for a day, a week, or even a month. Goodbye for a lifetime.

August 26, 1996

Your heaven birthday was yesterday. I was tense and distracted, but it wasn't the horrible day I was dreading. After a year of horrible days, the actual day was better than some days. We had our candle ceremony and then the balloons. Keegan's and Regan's (Rochelle's son) balloons got stuck in the tree so we figured you wanted them to hang out for awhile. It's hard . . . but it is getting easier. I am actually glad that one year has gone by now. Before, I didn't want time to pass. I just wanted time to stand still. Now, I want time to pass. I want to get further away from the sorrow and closer to feeling good again. I guess I am a changed person and I don't know what I will feel like in the future and what will "feel good." I know that I have become much more serious. Remember how I always used to be smiling? I don't do that anymore. Remember how you used to get frustrated with me when I was deep in thought and you were trying to get my attention?--well, that happens much more now.

I know I will never be able to feel like I can say "goodbye" to you, but I am beginning to feel like I can say "hello" to a future on earth without you. Even the thought makes me cry, but I can at least admit now that I can go on. I worry about Keegan, because I still don't think she understands or wants to understand. I know she has been blocking it out of her mind. The other night, she started thinking about your dog Sandy that ran away last summer. She cried terribly for Sandy saying how much she missed her. She had to have a picture to hold. Daddy tried talking to her about heaven and that she can see Sandy and you in heaven. She didn't want to talk about you. I think she is still denying. Yesterday, when we had the candle ceremony she was so serious but didn't cry. She sat there sucking her thumb and then said, "Mom, can I blow out the candles?" just like she had been ignoring the entire candle ceremony. Your cousin, Raina, had tons of questions about death, heaven, and where your body is. I didn't like hearing some of the questions.

Last week was a tough week--I kind of hit bottom. I went to the therapist which helped a lot. The therapist told me I need some "beginnings" in my life because I have had so many endings over the past year. She said to go to an exercise class or start some crafts. I know I haven't been taking care of myself because it has been so busy with all the kids around. I used to read each evening to keep myself "up" and I haven't had a chance to do that. I used to listen to tapes and I haven't been listening to my helping tapes. I used to work on crafts and I haven't been doing that. So . . . basically, I have been doing nothing to help myself feel better. The therapist told me to get some antidepressants from my doctor. I called to make an appointment for depression--and can you believe they said the first appointment they had was two weeks out? I told them I may not be depressed in two weeks and didn't make an appointment!! Why don't they treat depression as an emergency?--because it can be. There is so much in this world that I wish was "fixed." I guess that's why we can look forward to heaven so much.

Randy and the kids leave on Friday after Rochelle's treatment and then it will just be her. Randy and Regan will be back the next Friday, then September 9th is the big day of her scans. We should know then if the drug is working. Please, Please, Please!!!! Then, if it is working she and Regan will stay and Randy will go home. She and Regan will stay until the treatment becomes available in Minneapolis. She will probably just go home one week per month. It sounds like they may make the treatment available in Minneapolis but still leave her on the program in Tulsa. This will be such an answer to prayer if the drug is working. I think it is, because she looks better and I think she feels better. Although, she worries at the littlest pain and thinks her cancer is spreading. I am sure it is difficult for her to think positively, but she always thinks the worst.

Oh, Sweetie. Life is so strange--these twists of fate or whatever that causes such pain. Although I will never say, "Goodbye Kendrick," I can say, "I love you, I miss you, and I can't wait to see you again." Good night, Kendrick. I love you.

September 17, 1996

It all still seems like a very bad dream. Yesterday we had to sit through a day of depositions. Dad gave his deposition first, then I did, then two of the coaches. I was nervous, of course. It is hard to concentrate on the questions. Still I cannot believe this happened. It was so senseless. I told Dad that it seems like it will make me feel better if someone is to blame for this--but will I really feel better? At least it won't make me feel like I should have done something differently. I have so many "I wishes." I think the attorneys are going to recommend we drop the case. Unfortunately, in order to pierce the immunity of the school district and employees, we have to prove that the coaches basically knew that you could die and didn't care. I really don't believe that is the case. We will sit through two more coaches' depositions today, so we'll see what they say. It doesn't look good for a trial, though, and that may be better anyway. It just makes me so mad that you are gone. That we took you to practice, that we didn't send a snack (we didn't know), that we didn't send a sports drink, that Dad didn't check on you, that I gave you the allergy medicine, that any of this happened!!!!!!! Life is so hard now. It is still such a struggle to make it through each day. I can only pray, "Dear God, help me," most of the time because it is all too numbing to pray. I go through the day on remote pilot as best I can. If I am doing things that are routine, I make it through slowly. If I have to do something new, I struggle.

Rochelle's cancer has spread to her ribs, skull, sternum, humerus, and her liver has gotten worse. She did get approval to continue on the program at double the medicine dose for eight more weeks. She is still with us with just Regan, so things are quieter at the house.

Jenny McLaughlin spent the last two evenings with us because her mom and dad went out of town. Keegan slept down in her room with Jenny. I went down to kiss Keegan goodbye this morning and it reminded me of when I kissed you goodbye on August 7th. If only I wouldn't have left that day. I know I have to quit reliving the past. I can't have you back in this lifetime no matter what I do. But I am so ANGRY!!!

October 4, 1996

I have been a lot better the past couple weeks. I didn't take the depression medication, but I have been taking more vitamins and trying to read more and do positive activities like cross-stitching and listening to tapes.

I tried to call Sue Cauthen last evening and she was at a football game. It made me sad. Derrick is playing again this year. You should either be playing or watching. Jenny went last night too. I am being cheated. Oh, yes, I tell myself that you aren't being cheated. You are happy. You are in a great place. I hurt for me and I miss you. I am realizing more that this is a part of life. It isn't "why me?" for only the sadness. I need to ask "why me?" when I am being blessed, too. Now, I am feeling overwhelmed with Rochelle's sickness, too. I guess we are all dying, but she is looking like she is failing. I worry that she looks frailer. She tires easily. She and Regan left this morning to fly home. I think Dad will miss Regan, even though he will never admit that. Rochelle may bring Raina back with her instead. I really enjoy Raina, even though she can be a stinker. She is so sweet.

We met with the attorneys last Monday. It was like a big burden was lifted off me. They suggested we try to negotiate a settlement with the school making a donation to your foundation and helping us with a project through the foundation. I like that. I don't want to sue. I don't want to make anyone else feel bad. I just want to start working on positive activities. I want to help people. I don't like to see your coach feeling so bad. I know he should have given you water. But I can't wish him a bad life. We were suing only to make sure this doesn't happen to another child. The school was denying wrongdoing. Now they admit they should have done things differently. I like that we can move forward with the positive--if this works out. I guess it will if it's meant to be.

We're having a 40th anniversary celebration for Grandma and Grandpa Roseland on October 27th. I'm really not looking forward to going home for just a weekend and Grandma was mad we were *planning anything. It seems we just can't make her happy. I get so upset with her I can't even talk with her. She can take a positive and make it sound negative. I'm trying to choose to be happy and be positive, and when I talk to her she drags up any imaginable subject that can be neutral and maybe even positive and starts spiraling into the most tragic ending. Life has enough sadness without adding to it.*

The pictures of you that Uncle Rolland scanned to use as a "screen saver" on the computer are loaded now, so when we work at the computer the background is pictures of you. You're so lovely. Your spirit is lovely, too, which is what makes the memories so special. I know I will see you again so I have comfort in that. Great Uncle Art died on Tuesday--of course I know you know that--so you have another friend in heaven. He said that Allie (his wife) *appeared to him twice in a vision this past year since she died and said, "Art, this is great, you have to come up here." I really believe it is a better place, but it is the unknown that makes us apprehensive. So, we choose to hold onto this life and be fearful of death because we don't know for sure what lies ahead for us. I know when I see Christ and you it will be like a glorious morning.*

I love you, Kendrick.

March 6, 1997

Oh, my--a lot has happened since October 4th and I am feeling bad, so I know writing to you will help. Rochelle died on December 17th. They took her off the treatments in Tulsa in early November and didn't give her any options, so she went to Mexico for an experimental treatment. Randy seemed to think it would have worked had they gotten there sooner. Anyway, she had been retaining fluid in her abdomen since late October and it kept getting worse. She came back from Mexico in early December and went into the hospital.

She finally talked them into letting her go home and she went home on December 13th and died in her sleep on the 17th. Grandma was sitting next to her in bed when she died. Did you greet her? Her mind was failing towards the end so she couldn't express herself and I couldn't talk to her over the phone. I'm sure she knows how much I love her and how much I miss her.

Well, Dear, your foundation is now up and running. Our first meeting was on your birthday--February 5th. We are hoping to accomplish some activities this year that can make a difference. A coach/parent symposium is being planned for May, we will participate in the Kids' Health Fair at St. Mary's, and we will continue to distribute the water bottles and pamphlets.

Oh, you're having a little brother or sister in July. We are pretty excited, Keegan especially. She wants a sister. The ultrasound looked like a girl. I am having an amniocentesis on Monday to make sure there are no problems, because there was a slight abdominal dilation on the ultrasound that could be an indication of Down Syndrome. I just want to know one way or the other. I think I will find out the sex, too. Might as well know everything! Dad really wanted a son. He says he doesn't care, just so it is healthy, but I can tell. I think it will be easier having a girl because we would have a tendency to compare a son too much to you and that could be hard for the child.

I watched some videos on "negaholics" at work today. I took the test and was rated as a "confirmed negaholic." I know that is because I have been so beat up by life's circumstances. I struggled with self-confidence before and now I have been totally devastated by life and it is so hard to be "up." I was feeling down the other evening and I put in a positive tape to lift my spirits. Instead, I started bawling because the tape said things like, "You are where you are because of the choices you have made," and, "You made the decisions to get you to where you are." Dad asked what was wrong. I said I didn't want you to die, I don't want this baby to be sick, and I didn't want my career to fall apart. Well, I made it through the tapes and they started to help. I need to listen to positive tapes or read positive books, continually it seems, to keep from spiraling into the depths of despair.

I did okay when Rochelle died. I think it was worse when I found out she had cancer because I had to face the possibility of death. Now, I have dealt with that and with losing you, so it was easier when she died. I miss her, but she was getting so sick. I was feeling bad that she was in such pain and so unaware of the things she loved on this earth. I know she is just on a different plane now. Grandma and Robin said that she was probably organizing a birthday party on your birthday. I said you probably celebrate the going to heaven days rather than your earthly birthdays.

Well, I feel better already just talking with you. I need to assess my life, make my plan, and move forward. I think that begins by putting my job behind me and starting on the next phase of my life, which will be being a full-time mom for at least a year. That will be pleasant being home with Keegan and the baby. I really hope I don't have to go to work, unless I want to. I don't think I will ever be able to handle another high-level corporate job. I have changed too much and have become so much weaker. I am looking forward to writing a book about you and submitting articles about you to magazines. I hope I can succeed at that. I don't handle rejection well, so I wonder if I can get accepted on the first submission. Or will I be too scared of failing that I don't even submit?

Well, Honey, thanks for listening. You always were such a good listener.

Love, Mom

August 26, 1997

It's 4:30 a.m. I can't sleep. Yesterday it was two years. I ignore my sadness a lot now. I think about you, but I'm more peaceful about losing you. I guess that's acceptance? How could that ever be?!! In a way, I think it's more of the diversion of life away from my sorrow. At first I didn't want time to move. I thought life should just stand still until my grief was over. How could people around me go on living when I couldn't? Now, I feel like the more time that passes gets me closer to our reunion and further away from "that day." I feel good about having many happy days now. I think about you and then divert my thoughts many times to avoid the sadness. Like yesterday, we knew it was the two-year anniversary. We always do the candle memorial and balloons. The memorial always makes me cry. I really didn't want to cry or think too much about losing you. This year we had four balloons to send our love on to you.

Your sister, Rylee Rochelle, is here now. We think you met her in heaven before she came to earth to be with us. Did you? She is such a blessing. Dad wanted another son, but I think having a girl was best because a son would bring back painful memories and remind me even more of losing you. I still want a little brother for you, but I don't think I am ready. So, I'm glad Rylee is here--a little blessing to bring us some joy. We cried when she was born because she won't know you here on earth. I hope the videos, although so few, will stay good so we can show them to her. I think of the video of you from 1994 and I want to look at it, but I can't bring myself to watch it. I guess I'm avoiding the tears. I've never watched the funeral tapes either.

We went to Pride Night at the high school the other night. It's sad that you aren't a part of the teenage group and yet I still enjoy being around those activities that you would have been a part of. I guess I use my imagination that "this is what Kendrick would be doing." Dad and Aileah handed out the water bottles. The foundation is doing well and finally got the nonprofit IRS status. You'll have to send your thoughts on how we should be proceeding.

Chapter 8

I Can Live Again

It still hurts. The pain is still there. I can go days, weeks, and sometimes even months without crying, but then it hits. It may be a song or the sight of a person with his build or hair color. Sometimes it may bring a smile, sometimes it may bring a tear, and sometimes it may bring total, uncontrollable sobbing. But, I am living again. I can talk about him without making others uncomfortable. I can smile, I can laugh, and I can rush around with the rest of the world. I am living again because I have been filling up the emptiness with new joys in my life.

January 1, 1998

Life does go on—amazing—or so it seems. The baby interrupted my writing and now, here it is months later and a new year starting again without you. It is 12:05 a.m. We had a little New Year's welcome at 11:00 p.m. because Keegan was having trouble staying up. I still miss you terribly. I think of you many times each day. I don't cry often. The tears come to the edge of my eyes and I hold them back. I think I am tired of crying. We finally opened the door to your room a few months ago. It had been closed for two years. I need to clean it a little. It is very dusty. I don't like that—it seems even sadder with that layer of dust that shows the passing of time. It has been so long without you, but closer to when we'll meet again. Your sweet 16 birthday is coming up soon. How sweet it could have been. We still have the car that was supposed to be yours on your 16th birthday. We've had it up for sale for a year and only a couple of people have come to see it. Keegan doesn't want to sell it because of the memories with you in it. Remember our trip to Minnesota in it? I'm so glad we took that trip.

Another year begins without you but you are never far from our thoughts. Good night, Kendrick. I love you.

June 30, 1998

I'm sitting in bed, Keegan lying next to me with your Lion King t-shirt on and she is watching <u>Lion King</u>. She has been missing you terribly lately and talks about you a lot. So, tonight she wanted to wear one of your t-shirts to bed and then when she found the Lion King shirt she wanted to watch the movie too. The songs on it always make me a little sad.

We had another foundation meeting tonight. We had a good meeting—I would much rather have been home with you than attending a meeting in your memory. We got our shirts with the logo for the foundation and your name. Life is sure strange. I miss you a lot. Keegan has been saying a lot lately that she can't wait to get to heaven to see you. She wants to have some Lego's in her pocket when she sees you so you can play. She even can't wait to die so she can go to heaven to see you. We need her here more and hopefully the good Lord agrees.

December 23, 1999

Tomorrow is Christmas Eve and I'm still missing you each day and especially at the holidays. But, like always, I hold back the tears. I still worry that if I start crying I won't stop.

Your little brother that we wanted is here now. You know that, though, I'm sure—Brennan Kendrick. We wanted him to have your name in memory of his special big brother. He's such a joy to have. I'm glad we got another son. Each new blessing helps dull the pain and bring more joy in our lives to squeeze out the sadness.

Grandma and Grandpa Roseland were here for Thanksgiving and Rolland and his family, too. Now, Grandpa Fincher, Cindy and Coquet and Sheryl are here for Christmas. We've had more family around for the holidays since we moved to Arkansas. It is nice.

We opened family presents last night. Keegan wanted a CD player and when she opened it she was very excited and it reminded me of your last Christmas when you got the Sega game and you were so excited. We have the photo of your excited expression right after you opened it.

So much is happening in our lives. We're not standing still like we were—frozen with sadness. We're able to move forward and enjoy life more. I still have trouble in some areas and I become overwhelmed easily and can't concentrate like I used to. I think it was from the overwhelming stress of your illness, losing Rochelle and job problems. It was all too much and I'm still recovering but moving on. I'm even working part-time. I'd rather be a full-time mom but we need the money or else we'd have to sell the house. Your room is still there and I don't know if we'll ever be able to empty it. Even after all these years it just seems too final.

After Rylee was born I chose not to return to work. Personally it was the best decision, but financially it was more challenging. When Rylee was two years old I went to work part-time.

We're having Christmas dinner tomorrow and then going to church.

You'd be 18 in February and graduating this year. We're missing all those senior activities. We set up a scholarship in your memory through the foundation. We thought it would be appropriate to start it the year you would have been graduating.

Well, I intended to go to bed early with the baby. Seems strange to be 40 and have another infant. Grandma was a grandmother two times by this age. Now I have two little ones and Keegan. Keegan continues to be a special blessing to us. She's already 10—time goes fast.

I'm still so anxious to see you again. All this talk about Y2K and "the end" didn't bother me. I know we'll just all be together then and that would be awesome. I'm so happy with all four of my children and I'd love for all of us to be together.

Sleepy time . . . good night, Kendrick. I love you.

September 1, 2002

The last six weeks have been hard. You'd think after seven long years I'd be over the grief and on to happy memories. The loss is still too great. I especially have a hard time in January as I think of your February 5th birthday and then again starting in mid-July and through August since you left us in August. You would have been 20 this year. I know it is time to clean out your room—after all you'd be off at college and probably moved out anyhow. I went down there one night to start. I went through the funeral cards and the get well cards and spent hours looking through them and crying. I needed to do that I guess. Anyway the cards are in a box. Then I looked in your dresser—candy wrappers, miscellaneous stuff, socks, underwear. I couldn't even bring myself to throw out the candy wrappers, I thought —"that's some of the last candy Kendrick ate." Grandma and Grandpa Roseland sent money for me to buy a curio cabinet to put some of your things in. They knew I'd wanted to get one for a long time. So, it has a few things in it, and I'm waiting until I go through your room to fill the rest with happy memory things rather than sad funeral things.

Your little sister and brother really wear me out. Rylee is 5 and Brennan is 2 ½. They have way more energy than you and Keegan did. Keegan is great with them. I think she remembers what a great big brother you were and wants to be the same to Rylee and Brennan.

We didn't even release balloons on "the day" this year. It's too sad. Rylee found two pennies though and I told her that her big brother probably sent them to her. We had our canopies and water and mister at the "Frisco Days" in Rogers the day before "the day." It's the second year we've done that through the foundation and last year it was on the 25th. It's a good way to spend that day and weekend.

I've been angry again. I am still very mad. I still think it's all a dream sometimes, but I wonder what part is the dream and what part is reality. This world is just too painful sometimes.

I worked in the nursery at church a recent Sunday with a lady who had just found out the week before that her son had advanced cancer. The next Sunday in church she came and told me what a blessing I had been to her and that I had really helped her get through the week and that the new doctor was giving a better prognosis. I started to cry. I thought—"I don't want to be a blessing! Why can't I be blessed?" Then they started to sing "To God Be the Glory" in church and I was crying so much I thought I'd need to leave. That was the song I wanted at your "homecoming" party. We didn't get a party—we had to have a funeral. Your Aunt Rochelle even wrote a poem about that.

Where's My Party?

There was supposed to be a party,
A party for Kendrick.
Homecoming from the hospital,
His life would be a miracle.
There was supposed to be a party,
A party for Kendrick.
Celebrating his 14th birthday,
All his friends would come to play.
There was supposed to be a party,
A party for Kendrick.
Honoring his Confirmation Day,
Friends and relatives would come to pray,
There was supposed to be a party,
A party for Kendrick.
High School graduation was now here,
In his gown he would look so dear.
There was supposed to be a party,
A party for Kendrick.
College years have flown by,
And for a job he now applies.
There was supposed to be a party,
A party for Kendrick.
The bride and groom to be
Would have blessings from thee.
There was supposed to be a party,
A party for Kendrick.

A son was now born of their love,
Sent from heaven above.
There was supposed to be a party,
A party for Kendrick.
The big 4-0 was here,
2022 would be the year.
There was supposed to be a party,
A party for Kendrick.
And his wife of many years,
Would celebrate without any tears.
There was a party
A party for Kendrick.
But we were not invited
Because his party was held in heaven on August 25th.
(Rochelle Roseland Pederson)

I still have trouble focusing and my memory is weak. I think the trauma was too great. I ache for you. I can't believe it's been seven years. I can't believe I've made it seven years without you. I am angry I've had to live seven years without you. I am jealous of other people that get "miracles." I'm not angry at God, though. I'm just angry. Sometimes I'm a little angry at the situations and people that contributed to your death—and that includes me for letting you play football, not being better prepared and having you better prepared, and for going out of town that day. I get mad at Dad thinking maybe if he would have recognized what was happening . . . coaches, school system—you name it—I can be angry at all of them. But it doesn't change a thing. I don't have you.

I only have memories. Sometimes I can barely stand the heartache and pain of losing you. Other times the memories are so sweet I forget the pain. Most of the time I'm just so caught up with life pushing me forward—sometimes dragging me—that I can't stop to grieve or savor the memories.

Keegan started eighth grade at Elmwood this year. That's probably why I'm having a hard time. She's your age, starting the grade you couldn't start. It was hard to get used to, but the counselor was very kind and understanding. Just knowing someone understands helps. Keegan is a sweet and beautiful 13 year old--just as you were sweet and handsome. I'm glad she remembers you so we can share stories. One day Rylee even said, "I miss my big brother Kendrick." I guess we talk about you so much that she even misses that you are not here.

One day at a time. I still miss you and love you deeply, my dearest Kendrick. Good night, Kendrick. I love you. XOXOXOXOX. Thank goodness your little brother and sister like to give and receive hugs and kisses.

Chapter 9

Fifteen Years Later

December 9, 2010

Dear Kendrick,

Over eleven years since I have written to you. Even though you are not here with me in person, you are still a part of my life. As I write on these pages I remember all the nights I wrote to you almost paralyzed with fear to face another night and another morning. But time did not stand still. Time kept moving and dragging me along with it. Moments turned into hours, hours into days, days into weeks, weeks into months, months into years, and here I am over fifteen years after you died and still wondering how I got through it. How did I get through those days?! They were so hard. Sometimes I get angry, sometimes I get sad, sometimes I smile fondly, sometimes I cry, but mostly I just realize that life needs to be lived and I can either live it or let it pass me by. The hard days became fewer and fewer and now I find that most of my days are filled with much joy and happiness.

Your little sister, Keegan, is 21 years old and was married last year. She married a nice man, Greg. I think you would have liked him as a brother-in-law. He is really good to Keegan and he has a wonderful family that Keegan is now a part of and we have another great son in our family.

Rylee is 13 and reminds me a lot of you. She has some of your mannerisms and is going to be tall like you. Brennan is 11 and has your sense of humor. I kept trying to convince him to play baseball and I never could get him interested in that. I used to love going to your baseball games.

Your dad and I divorced three years ago. Some people think losing a child increases the chance of divorce, but, in our case, I think it held us together longer. That was another hard challenge to get through. I do not need any more challenges.

The Kendrick Fincher Hydration Foundation continues to keep me busy. I have been "employed" there full time since your dad and I divorced. We changed the "memorial" to "hydration" to better identify our mission. I still don't like that I have to do this. I still wish you were here. There was another child that died from heat stroke in Arkansas this year. I feel bad because we haven't been able to do more.

Well, Honey, this has been a hard road. Certainly not one I would have chosen. But, what road would I have chosen? I guess that is why we make the best choices we can in life because there is still so much left to chance.

I love you, Kendrick. You will always be in my heart and on my mind. I would rather have been attending your high school graduation, college graduation, wedding and rocking your babies than fundraising, doing hydration presentations and planning events. One of these days, Sweetie, I will feel like I have done all I could. One day during the time Daddy and I were divorcing

I was crying and I told the kids I just couldn't do it anymore. I remember Rylee and Brennan putting their hands on my back as I was sobbing and they said, "Mommy, you can't quit the foundation." So, I continue for Keegan, for Rylee, for Brennan and all the other children that have benefited from your legacy. I don't think I do it for you. I don't have you. I guess I mostly do it for other children's parents because they don't deserve to lose a child to something preventable. I am doing what I wish someone else would have done so I didn't have to lose you.

I think we have made a difference, though. Over 225,000 children have received a squeeze bottle with your name on it, your name has been on all the NFL websites even though you never got to play one day of football, your name is in the Congressional Record from when August was designed Heat Stroke Awareness month in 2008, and there is so much more.

I still don't know why you had to die. What I do know is that I get to choose to find the joy that is in each day and embrace that. Some days that joy is very hard to find, but if I look really hard there is always joy to be found. And, as this day closes, I get to tell you again . . . good night, Kendrick. I love you. Always and forever I love you.

My final chapter is still being written. Someone has said that we are where we are in life by the choices we make. Well, I did not choose for Kendrick to die. I did not choose to be divorced at 48. I did not choose for my sister to die. Her kids did not choose to live without their mother. Wait! We are where we are in life by the choices we MAKE. There are many things that happen in our life that we would not choose to HAPPEN. But we can MAKE the choice to live or we can MAKE the choice to remain in our grief. Your child's life has reached its finale. But you have a life to live. Live it so that your child would be proud. You have the choice to design your final chapter.

The Kendrick Fincher Hydration (Memorial) Foundation

A portion of the proceeds from the sale of this book will benefit the Kendrick Fincher Hydration Foundation. For more information on the Kendrick Fincher Hydration Foundation you can view the website at www.kendrickfincher.org.

Vision

Improved safety for athletes and a reduction in the number of injuries and death from heat related causes for all ages.

Mission

Promote proper hydration and prevent heat illness through education and supporting activities.

Values

We Believe,
- Children should have adequate access to water throughout the school day to maintain proper hydration
- Athletes should have frequent water/sports drink breaks
- Athletes should be able to get a drink at any time during practices

- Coaches should be trained in heat illness prevention and emergency procedures
- Parents should understand their child's hydration needs and encourage proper hydration

Education and Supporting Activities

- Presentations to school aged children on the importance of proper hydration
- Presentations to athletes, coaches and parents on proper hydration and heat illness prevention
- Distribution of squeeze bottles and educational pamphlets to support our educational presentations
- Representation at health fairs to educate the public about our mission and activities
- Community involvement in support of our mission by providing "cool huts"—misting tents with free ice water—at various outdoor public events.
- Annual free youth run in Rogers, AR, to reinforce our mission and help children learn about the importance of proper hydration and physical fitness in a fun environment.
- Hydration campaign to educate parents, coaches and athletes on heat illness prevention (www.hydrationcampaign.com).

How we accomplish our mission (funding)

- Annual Fund Drive
- Corporate Partnerships
- Sustainable funding: hydration campaign, resources
- Fundraisers including our signature event the Kendrick Fincher Youth Run

Thank you to . . .

God, for the strength and courage to face each new day.

Rey Hernandez, my friend who kept asking me, "How is your book coming along?" with enough persistency and encouragement to make me get it done.

My friends and family that share the experience of losing a child and read the manuscript to provide feedback and suggestions: Brandi Ellzey, Rey Hernandez, Warren Jones, and John and Darlene Roseland.

Book reviewers Scarlett Daniels, Jerri Dwyer, Robin Langevin, and Mary Roseland.

Those that were my rock and support during the time Kendrick was in Little Rock: the Customer Service Team; my friend, Sandy Miller, who has since joined Kendrick in heaven; my mom, Darlene Roseland, who stayed at the hospital with us; Robert and Cindy Fincher; Sheryl Fincher; and all the family and friends who called, visited, or sent notes.

Mike Fincher, the father of my children who shared the sorrow of losing a child with me.

Keegan Fincher Ball, my daughter that held my hand and cuddled with me many nights when all I could do was cry or sit in a zombie-like state. She now shares wonderful memories of her brother with me.

Rylee Fincher, my daughter born two years after Kendrick died and helped bring much joy and laughter into my life and home.

Brennan Fincher, my son born four years after Kendrick died who provided the joy of more hugs, kisses, and Lego's around the house.

Amy MacArthur, the friend from work that helped me plan and prepare the details for Kendrick's funeral. I will never forget her kindness.

Tammy Murabito, the friend from work that helped in our early transition to our 18 days in Little Rock.

Sue Cauthen, our friend from Rogers that brought us warm clothes to wear in the cold hospital and shared a very hard night with us and for her many kind actions during and after the hospital stay.

Sherry Sieber and the Customer Service Team for setting up the bank account that ended up being the seed funds for the Kendrick Fincher Memorial Foundation.

Dr. George Schaefer who was the first physician to treat Kendrick when he arrived at the hospital, served on the Board of Directors of the Kendrick Fincher Memorial Foundation for nine years, started the Kendrick Fincher Youth Run and continues as run director.

The doctors and nurses at Arkansas Children's Hospital for working so hard to try save Kendrick's life and for their compassion to our family.

Our relatively new neighbors in Arkansas who helped in any way they could.

The community of Rogers, Arkansas for the support and kindness showed to the "newcomers" who lost a child.

My many friends who have provided laughter and friendship over the years to help me keep filling up my life with pockets of joy.

My family and extended family for the memories shared and comfort provided.

Friends, volunteers, and supporters of the Kendrick Fincher Hydration Foundation that are helping keep children and athletes safe.

Additional Resources

I spent a lot of time reading to help me through the grieving process. Here is a list of some of the books that I read that you may also find beneficial.

Bramblett, John. *When Good-Bye is Forever: Learning to Live Again after the Loss of a Child*. New York: Ballantine, 1991.

Connelly, Douglas. *After Life: What the Bible Really Says*. Illinois: InterVarsity Press, 1995.

Cox-Chapman. The *Case for Heaven: Near-Death Experiences as Evidence of the Afterlife*. New York: G. P. Putnam's Sons, 1995.

Fitzgerald, Helen. *The Mourning Handbook: The Complete Guide for the Bereaved*. New York: Simon and Schuster, 1994.

Graham, Billy. *Angels: God's Secret Agents*. Dallas: Word Publishing, 1994.

Graham, Billy. *Death and the Afterlife*. Dallas: Word Publishing, 1987.

Holmes, Marjorie. *To Help You Through The Hurting: A Loving Guide to Faith, Hope and Healing*. New York: Bantam, 1984.

Johnson, Barbara. *Pain is inevitable but Misery is Optional: So, Stick a Geranium in Your Hat and Be Happy!* Dallas: Word Publishing, 1990.

Kubler-Ross, Elisabeth. *Death: The Final Stage of Growth.* New Jersey: Prentice-Hall, 1975.

Kushner, Harold S. *When Bad Things Happen to Good People.* New York: Avon Books, 1981.

Peale, Norman Vincent. *Why I Believe in Life Beyond Death.* Michigan: Zondervan, 1996.

Steiger, Brad and Sherry Hansen. *Children of the Light: Children's Near-Death Experiences and how they Illumine the Beyond.* New York: Signet, 1995.

Tatelbaum, Judy. *The Courage to Grieve: Creative Living, Recovery and Growth Through Grief.* New York: Harper and Row, 1980.

Taylor, Rick. *When Life is Changed Forever: By the Death of Someone Near.* Oregon: Harvest House Publishers, 1992.

Van Praagh, James. *Healing Grief: Reclaiming Life After Any Loss.* New York: New American Library, 2001.

White, Mary A. *Harsh Grief Gentle Hope.* Colorado: NavPress, 1995.

Wiersbe, David W. *Gone But Not Lost: Grieving the death of a Child.* Michigan: Baker Book House, 1992.

Zunin, Leonard M. and Hillary Stanton. *The Art of Condolence: What to Write, What to Say, What to Do At a Time of Loss.* New York: Harper Collins, 1991.

Photos

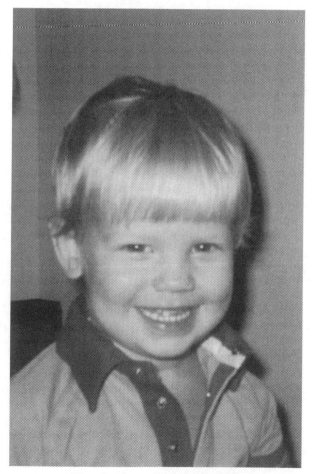

Kendrick at 18 months old

Kendrick at 5 years old

Proud big brother Kendrick with little sister Keegan.
He was six years old and she was two months old.

Me with Kendrick when he was 10 and Keegan was 3

Kendrick at 12 years old with his dad at Disneyland

One of my favorite photos of Kendrick and Keegan
taken in December 1994

Kendrick's last Christmas.   He was so excited to get the Sega Genesis.

Kendrick's birthday #13 . . . his last to share with us.

Our last photo of me and Keegan with Kendrick taken as
we were leaving Minnesota at the end of July

My family today: Me with Keegan and her
husband Greg, Rylee and Brennan

Rhonda Fincher earned bachelor's and master's degrees from Regis University in Denver. She is co-founder and Executive Director of the Kendrick Fincher Hydration Foundation, which educates children, athletes, and parents on the importance of proper hydration and heat illness prevention. She continues to live and work in Rogers, Arkansas.